Praise for *The Terribly Beautiful*
2006 MAIN STREET RAG EDITOR'S CHOICE CHAPBOOK SERIES

Gritty, erotic, and sublime, these poems by Darius Stewart embody the truth and beauty that Keats claimed we need to know to survive. The honesty, precision, warmth and lyrical mystery move us, show us more about what it means to be human. In these poems we recognize the beautiful contradictions, that beauty and the world are not incompatible. The poems are prescient, they see waves and rubble, and what can be salvaged with skilled hands and imagination. What has been rescued is here, in these precise and memorable words.

—Marilyn Kallet (Circe, After Hours)

"The beauty of / how gracefully heat dances before the eyes," perfectly reflects the essence of Darius Stewart's opulent debut chapbook collection. Here notions of beauty appear and reappear, intensely renewed at each turn by Stewart's technical grace and open-hearted acts of witness. As the paradoxical title suggests, these poems breathe at the crossroads of anguish and joy, desire and experience. *The Terribly Beautiful* is a brave and intimate, finely wrought premiere. What a pleasure to read the work of a young poet who will no doubt continue to electrify us for years to come.

—Terrance Hayes (Hip-Logic - National Poetry Series Selection)

In *The Terribly Beautiful*, Darius Stewart explores desire—from the poignant to the sublime, from the suggestive to the frank and direct. In his self-portraits and portraits of others, the human body in all its grief, sensuality, and passion is revealed as nothing short of heroic. Darius Stewart is a poet of both brash and subtle gifts.

—Denise Duhamel (Queen for a Day: Selected and New Poems)

There is a rare elegance in these moving poems by Darius Stewart, a delicacy driven by the speaker's passion for a felt life, a passion so acute the work becomes textural—Keats and his rich palette. Underlying these poems, quietly, is the raw effort "to understand the grief" of loss and self-discovery, all of it conducted under the ever-present threat of HIV and AIDS in the life of being a young gay Black man. From the young boy lost in the woods, to his understanding of how the past is threaded through a blue silk robe, these poems muscle up to the hard work of learning how to live with dignity and inner strength in a ruthless world. *The Terribly Beautiful* marks the introduction of an important new voice, one that has earned its compassion and intelligence.

—Arthur Smith (The Late World)

What lovely, luscious, luxurious poems are written by Darius Stewart! They restore us to the deliciousness of language and experience. I bask in their intelligence and their beauty, with gratitude.

—Naomi Shihab Nye (19 Varieties of Gazelle: Poems of the Middle East)

Praise for *Sotto Voce*
2008 MAIN STREET RAG EDITOR'S CHOICE CHAPBOOK SERIES

Darius Stewart has crafted poems that are sincere, intimate, disturbing, funny, and sad. He shows us how the ordinary becomes poetry and how poetry becomes music. To the Italians, "sotto voce" is an expression meaning to speak under one's breath. Stewart speaks to us in a hushed voice, but it arises out of "a vicious house / of ghosts // that haunt." The spirit of these poems is gentle. But the impact is fierce.

—Hayan Charara (*The Sadness of Others*)

"One can perform pirouettes in sensible shoes, / though we prefer the spangled ones." In *Sotto Voce*, Darius Stewart documents the passionate rush of male-on-male sex; the heartbreak of hitting false notes in love; and the dangerous gaze of a boyhood spent observing men's bodies "glisten[ing] like rhinestones mined from a cave / deep within our ghetto." These complex and graceful lyrics move effortlessly from "queen palms, / where herons rustle" to "the well-lit savage part of the city," detailing natural and urban pleasures, domestic and sensual mysteries. This is a subversive, elegant collection that merits reading and re-reading.

—Carol Guess (*Femme's Dictionary*)

In *Sotto Voce*, Darius Stewart's second chapbook collection, are poems that explore physical (and metaphysical) connections (and barriers): here is a deeply attentive gaze that uncovers signs and omens everywhere. The subject, of course, is longing, and the language is nuanced, tender, organic yet often surprisingly fresh in its precise rendering of moments and metaphors.

—Ron Mohring (*Survivable World*)

Praise for *The Ghost the Night Becomes*
2013 GERTRUDE PRESS POETRY CHAPBOOK CONTEST WINNER

The truth is we are all dying, and the desire to be mourned and remembered is as tactile as a lump in the throat when one is nervous, or falling in love. The poems in *The Ghost the Night Becomes* are every bit as complicated and visceral: private and confessional, lyrical and narrative, elegiac and celebratory. Darius Stewart's poems reflect a world where a man with a tattoo of a tear on his right cheek is "...not / one given to sentimentality—a perpetual crier—but he's a murderer..." Still, there is hope. These are songs of lament meant to soothe the inevitable loss of love, sexuality, trust, and life; but they are also a balm, an attempt to confront and remedy the paradoxical need for human connection. In "A Tryst" two men meet at a motel for a "...quick fuck that never happened." But lust is only the occasion, and the speaker notes that it's "a small price to pay / simply to be beside him / covers pulled up to my chin, waiting out the night." The same night where, in the title poem, "some living thing cocks its ear & knows / that in this forest a boy is lost, & the trail he's making, some dead thing is covering it up." In moments that confront with absolute self-awareness both the desire to hold onto and be held by another, Stewart glimpses the beautiful truth of our mortality. No matter how hard we try, "we bury not only the dead but the living."

—Dexter L. Booth (*Scratching the Ghost*)

Reading these poems is like listening to the blues while driving alone at night down some lost country road. *The Ghost the Night Becomes* entwines sex and desire, violence and loss, in unforgettable, haunting ways. The poems are tender and deeply human, and the language is lush. Stewart's elegies follow you like ghosts "wrist-bound to one another."

—Ansel Elkins (*Blue Yodel* - 2014 winner, Yale Series of Younger Poets)

In *The Ghost the Night Becomes*, Darius Stewart remembers and pays tribute to the ghosts of the dead and the living. His words are delicate, powerful, and often eerily intimate. In "The Cellist's Lament," addressed to Matthew Shepard, Stewart writes, "I embrace this instrument / as if it were your body dying / in a forest of no trees, only leaves to prove they once existed." Just as the leaves make the absence of the trees impossible to ignore, Stewart's words make it impossible to ignore those memories and voices which have faded into silence.

—Allison Tobey, Poetry Editor, Gertrude Press

Intimacies in Borrowed Light

poems

Darius Stewart

drawings by
Annie Fletcher

EastOver Press
Rochester, Massachusetts

Intimacies in Borrowed Light

Darius Stewart

POETRY

ISBN 978-1-958094-01-3

~

Book Design: **EK Larken**
Cover Design: **Shelly O'Barr**
Interior Drawings: **Annie Fletcher**
Content Editor: **Jesse Graves**
Assistant Content Editor: **Sappho Stanley**

Shelly O'Barr's cover design is based on
a photograph by **Joshua McKnight.**

~

PUBLISHED IN THE UNITED STATES OF AMERICA BY

EASTOVER
— PRESS —

Rochester, Massachusetts

www.EastOverPress.com

In memory of my father
CLARENCE ("SNOOK") EUGENE STEWART III
February 2, 1962-May 23, 2022

Contents

~ Part I ~

~ Part II ~

~ PART III ~

ILLUSTRATIONS

Part I

Murophobia

manifested on one of those too-hot-to-go-outdoors days
when Daddy gave my brother & me watermelon

slices to keep us cool in the heat. We let the
juice run like sweat all the way down to our chins,

a sticky mess for two damn-near, grown-ass boys.
Meanwhile, Daddy left us for nips off the bottle.

We were his breathalyzers, so we knew how much liquor
limbered his efforts to go "hard as a motherfucker"

getting rats off traps in the basement. He'd bring us down
to show us how to do it ourselves, teach us not to be afraid

to dispose of what would have tried to kill us first.
This was his tour in Desert Storm talking, the booze,

or thrill of the kill, who knows? We were twelve & ten
& tightened fists in acts of resistance. Instinctively, to gaze upon

a snarled, triangular face conjured images of a rat's fangs,
not our own fingernails, scoring the insides of our palms.

Daddy made us kneel in observance of the one rat caught
at the very top of the basement stairs. It was chief among the others,

the marauder of darkness whose whiskers had failed him.
It hedged its bets creeping along the baseboards until

it mistook peanut butter on a block for an easy meal.
There's no such thing as a free lunch & now

it stared back at us with eyes dark as two periods.
Daddy beamed father-son bonding with his boys.

One of us had to remove it, though. Snap back metal pinning
a rat's neck to a wedge of wood & yank it by its tail.

The other held open an empty grocery bag & felt the weight of death
plopped in. We saved money on traps by saving the traps.

The grocery bag interring the body was the least we could do
to dignify its life. No prayer was spoken over the dead except

let this be a lesson to the others. Daddy kept more traps
farther down in darker corners of the basement

& led us to them. They were empty with the ghosts
of the absent dead. & later that night, as I slept,

I felt a presence waft scantly across my arm.
With the opposite hand, I touched what seemed

a mischievous scuttle bristling the fine hairs.
Over & over I turned until startled awake frightened

when I saw in the hallway light
glowing beneath my bedroom door

the last of its hindfeet & tail
vanishing through a sliver in the wall.

Self-Portrait at Eight

Once, as I tiptoed across the cold tile floor
of the apartment, to the bathroom, peeking
in the adjacent room, I saw my mother naked.
She slept tethered to my father, oblivious
to my wonder. Breasts rose from her,
peaked with coal-black nipples
never used for suckling. I stood amazed.
My first look at the female body.
Years later, while having sex
for the first time, I wondered
if seeing my mother's body awash
in early morning light, hearing her
slow, rumbling breath fill the room, is
what beckoned me to the man.

Picaresque

Yes, even teenaged boys kiss their pillows
as they've known their sisters to do.
I was no exception.

Only the pictures of mannequin-perfect women
on my walls that most boys would pretend
love-making—their slinky blue dresses bunched

around their waists, just barely covering their asses
like sagging skin—was more my brother's
predilection than mine—since secretly

I fantasized about the boys
on the basketball court playing within
the chain-linked fence. Their shirts off, skins

glistened like rhinestones mined from a cave
deep within our ghetto. Their bodies swayed—
one hand gripping net-less hoops—ripened

in twilight as though any moment
they'd tattoo themselves to night's papyrus.
Surely this was girlhood whimsy: each night

sinking my head into the cold
pillow cushion dreaming of asses
barely contained in jeans they pulled up

sporadically as if to showcase the bulbous
curves with no more shame
than women on my walls cocking enough

leg to send any other boy into a frenzy.
But my glee manifested in those sweat-grimed
boys scaling fences erected

like prison bars around the neighborhood while cops chased them into a choke-
hold. I'd watch just as any nosy neighbor too bored

with their own life to pay attention to it:
how they writhed beneath grips
as they'd done a thousand times before

wrestling with other boys—almost like a rite
of passage in case, one day, they'd have to
fight themselves out of juvenile hall, or worse,

prison... which is what I felt
I was living in each time
D & I sat on the bus bench for no

particular reason other than to hear
D's stories of sticking two fingers in
a girl's vagina because I had to,

because D couldn't help but be
the only one of us teenage boys to fuck
a girl & have us withering

in the fire of his telling, as if he were
behind the pulpit speaking the gospel
of how boys became men who fuck

as if fucking were a sacrament
meant to dissolve on the tongue.
In his gaze I became a specter

of a once-present thing. I was
no longer there—if only to fall prey
to my own self-consciousness:

remembering I was caught once
prancing around in fluffy pink slippers,
claiming to be queen of my own parade.

My father stood there in the doorjamb
with smoke coiling around his eyes
because I was that hot, or else

he refused to believe his own son could be
a faggot. For years I pretended to be
one of D's boys, though it couldn't last.

It became more difficult to escape
men like ghosts wandering parks
in light bare enough to see lips moving

like ventriloquists beckoning me
to touch, to kneel down not in prayer
but for the promise of one's body: one man

becoming the second skin of another, to be
unafraid of cock-in-hand-becomes-mortar-&-pestle.
I could've screamed as if a mouthful of wasps

had escaped & tried to cut myself
from that scene. Except I'd become
too comfortable there in the shadows,

where slivers of light revealed
bodies ravishing in silhouette
panting, eager, & waiting.

Saleem & Son's Barbershop

Among the rubble of buildings
the length of Magnolia Avenue
is a store-front shop with prison bars
protecting cracked glass.
Inside, clippers edge lines in heads
that emerge from black sheets draped
across chests. The counter behind them
is a sea of lotions, soap-cakes, pomades:
things that make men beautiful.
A television set blares rap videos of girls
with wide hips & phat asses that jook jive & shake
to a beat of songs stolen
from the lives past of men sitting beneath the razor—
exclaiming just how wide, how phat.
I wait my turn in the chair, smile at their remarks.
I need to be summoned to the chair,
where I will sit, feel the shaving away
of hair transformed into something beautiful
like music of men cackling & high-five smacking palms.

The Terribly Beautiful

To say this is the story of our lives.
Who is to say there is a story at all?
To be enchanted by a tune—
"Clair de Lune" from *Suite Bergamasque*—
when we complain moonlight pales
finer features of a disrobed body:
your sinewy muscles, my clumsy limbs.
To endure amaryllis blossoms season after season,
but a fly's life will last no longer
than the passing of one hour to the next.
To be a river that empties into the gulf,
& the gulf that destroys land
on which our houses are built.
To misunderstand the world we grieve.
To understand the grief.

Necessary Vanity
after Annette Bening

If having your heart
broken is a tremendous way
    to learn about the world
    then why be ashamed to wish
falling in love can be the same
as staring into a mirror
    after a fresh haircut
    enamored by clean
razor-sharp edges
which rewards a face its depth—
a mustache & goatee
    perfectly yoked
    framing a mouth supple
turned mischievous grin
when subsumed by
    such a vision?

One becomes almost obsolete
the way falling in love is
    surely a manner of casting
    the old self into the damnable void
to see the new self more deliberately
insisting to be worth more
    than simple beauty
    more than ridding hair
that once kinked up the skull
hair that is swept away in neat strokes
    to be banished to the trash heap.

Why not wish falling in love
will be precisely this way
    when one feels a once familiar hand trace
the contours of a showroom new head
entirely with eyes closed in *la la*
imagining it is his touch always
    his & only
    him there behind you
swooning.

Driftwood

The hours when a young sun grows old,
shade encroaches over the maple trees.
We sit hunched over
beneath porch-board planks. Down here
is a cavern so black our skins glow
iridescent. Splinters hang like stalactites
& graze the curve of our spines.
We've done this every night for so long—
crossed legs crush grass & weeds
pummeling through the earth. We are
hiding from the straight boys
moving above our heads. We hear them whisper
where are they? They spread into the yard
as though wolves scavenging the plains, waiting
until the sun slowly dies behind the moon.
No light can show our neon skins,
only their glowing, hollow eyes.
I arch my body over his, or his over mine,
& we take turns massaging aches from our bodies.
When finally they return to the house,
the ear of the moon guides us from underneath the porch,
past the maple trees to a lake where we can sit
along the shore to watch small rippling tides.
We reach for driftwood & cast it back.
We wish it was large enough to carry us.

Dusk

after Amaud Jamaul Johnson

begins with simple house cats
crouched
behind the queen palms,
where herons rustle
water's edge, a pond
giving up
the mountain ridges,
reflecting shades
of pink & each cat
indistinguishable
from the other,
though there is light
enough to see each feline
belly-crawl
through short grasses—
this sight so beholden
to hints of rain
tracing the air
with scents of spring,
the sky the pale cheek
of herons unsuspecting
two cats
creeping along
the grass like clouds
before the gathering
of storms.

Self-Portrait in a Thunderstorm

I've been brooding in the swelter,
awaiting a tremendous downpour, for

thunderclaps to shudder the still
air the way a man's thighs

flex & tremble
during sex. I'm not a difficult man to please.

I sit bunkered in the foxhole
sniffing for evaporated water rising

in the air, listening for rain
on pavement, to flood the eaves,

for cataracts to split into streams down the side
of the house, to collect in puddles on the lawn,

to make music more beautiful than fish
flinging acrobatic bodies all

rainbow & mouth from dark water,
but more fleeting than a thousand coins of light

vanishing into deep, black pools.
But the days continue to billow

with no storms, a season of smoke & ash.
I want to descend into illusion, a thicket of dreams

where water rushes for a precipice, & thunder
echoes in grottoes carved into earth, reaching

worlds unknown. I won't awaken
from this sleep. I want to be whatever pulls itself

to the bank, steps upon the grass to marvel
at the world only thunder will beckon from its own.

Self-Portrait with Dog

In a bed of green grass the dog dozes.

As if rowing the sky overcast
her legs paddle air, & where

there is sunlight filtering in, she is
radiant. Her coat of fur newly washed is soft
as cotton swabs I use to cleanse her ears,
the corners of her eyes where sleep has congealed
into a stubborn mucus.

Watching her is like air threatening
a menacing storm, as now she growls
in her sleep, her feet still a fretwork
of activity, as if escaping a mob
vengeful against her sharp bite,
as if she is from a lineage of dogs
snarling on the same side of a water hose's blast.

But what does she know of those times?

Her ears perk at shrapnels of noise.

Is it the sound of skin split open,
spilled blood in the concrete cracks
lugging on its back what has been wasted
to the gutters?

My knowledge of history becomes a language
translated by her nervous whimpering, &

unprovoked her body trembles

as I tremble
when anyone walks
across the future site
of my grave.

Reverb at the Carousel II
Knoxville, Tennessee

I admire drag queens who decorate themselves
in gold ropes   hoops of silver   hair up & splayed
faces blushed with pastels   luminous in their evening gowns
they carry themselves with as much femininity as a mayor's wife
their bodies jingling across a dance floor like scattered coins
I'm too shy to consider such a thing   a novice so green
I don't know the difference between a drag king & a drag queen
I cross my arms over the other in the customary stance of confusion
when I witness a spectacle of shimmering bodies lost in beats of the music's
thousand hearts   I wish my passion for this scene will never be extinguished
& after some time & less bashful I allow a boy to grind me
his eyes ask me to wrap my fingers around his cock but I ignore them
I breathe the musk of him   I prefer he begs to take me home
& croon me to sleep   keep me on edge of a dream with his soft breathing
one arm wrapped around my chest   a hand cupping the roundest parts
of my body as he enters the various splits   whispering wet into my ear

Whispering wet into my ear   he entered the various splits
while a hand cupped the roundest parts of my body
one arm wrapped around my chest kept me on edge
of a dream   with his soft breathing he crooned me to sleep
I preferred that he beg to take me home so I could breathe the musk of him
his eyes asked me to wrap my fingers around his cock
but I ignored them   & after some time & less bashful
I allowed this boy to grind me   I wished my passion for this scene
would never be extinguished   witnessed a spectacle of shimmering bodies
lost in beats of the music's thousand hearts   I crossed my arms
over the other in the customary stance of confusion   I didn't know
the difference between a drag king & a drag queen   I was too shy to consider
such a thing   a novice so green I simply watched them jingle their bodies
across a dance floor like scattered coins   they carried themselves
with as much femininity as a mayor's wife   these drag queens with faces
blushed in pastels   luminous in their evening gowns   hair up & splayed
decorated in gold ropes & hoops of silver

Self-Portrait on a Key West Auction Block
for Tyson

Here, a roomful of frat boys scrambles to pluck each petal of my body, hoping to make my cock blossom. The auctioneer quiets them, begins the bidding at $50 *(& who'll give me 60... do I hear 70...)* & on up until he says *Sold for $500 to the five boys from...* I'm their mandingo, their I've-never-been-with-a-black-man man, & their anxious faces flush with expectation, break into grins as though wondering *is it true what they say?...* I focus my attention on the group of boys in the back standing with tented hands across their bulging crotches, paralyzed by their own beautiful reticence. Those boys are what I once was—curious, afraid: dance with lesbians because it's safe, hide in shadows witnessing pockets of men gyrating against another, wrapped in indigo glow. They hate this song, or love it in private, & question what goes on behind curtains, or in the farthest rooms marked off with velvet ropes. I'm sure tonight they will go home, lie in bed, tremble from one hand's manual labor, & one day, perhaps, they'll be heaved on a block such as this one. Gaze at oil slicked bodies & later have sex that will end with no alarms or bells, cigarettes or half-full pints of beer. & each boy will collect articles of clothing from backs of chairs, windowpanes, bedposts, & will leave, head bowed. The same way I will be when I'm led down the plank by the arms, the torso. Shuffling past faces my eyes will never see stamped with insidious grins.

After Rene Magritte's "The Lovers"

She knows how important it is to inspect cantaloupes
for her husband, who prefers them softer

than the produce manager allows,
so she stores them in the pantry

for several days until the fruit gives way
to her gentle squeeze. *And that is what love is,*

she thinks on those evenings when she sits in his company
beside a fire as he reads his newspaper,

a tumbler of J&B clenched in his fist, & she, a glass
of cherry wine, sitting cross-legged,

questioning everything the shadows hide
from her: dark circles around

her eyes, gray wisps of hair tangled in black.
She does not bother him with these frivolities,

but dangles her legs
like pairs of earrings he buys

to reassure her they will remember love,
know it every day & awaken each morning

one warm body curving around the other.
She is content with that,

knows love is varied & tacit
as gardenias blossoming with her careful tending,

or the cat purring around his feet
for a scratch behind the ears.

Love through touches: he brushes her hair & bathes her
in the half-dusk; she holds his face

in cupped palms while he whispers prayers of thanks
for seeing the world unfurling:

birds unmoored in their prairie of sky, returning
to nest, wing-worn. The way lovers prolong sleep, eager

for the moon's bright bloom to wrap them in sheets
of light, where they rest against one another

before an open window, listening for some trace in the air:
a cat's purr, gardenias unfolding their petals.

Semantics
Is there such a thing as unrequited friendship?
—*J. D. McClatchy*

There is such a thing as unrequited friendship.
It masquerades as love.

When I mean to say I'm in love with you
I tell him, *I love you.*

He smiles, says: *I love you, too.*
You're like a brother to me.

Respond: *I love you more than my luggage.*
Love you like a play cousin—

"play" meaning "pretend"
because I love from a distance, make believe

I don't care he means love differently from me.
I write it off, continue to mock love.

Mouth *elephant juice.*
He laughs, slaps my thigh, leans in close.

I take the opportunity. Remove a stray hair
I noticed earlier on his shirt. I save it

in my wallet with others I've collected.
In time I'll have his whole oily head in there.

for M.O.

Aubade

If love is a beautiful thing
      why won't it sing
a praise song
      to the body: my tongue's
route of his inner mouth, wet
      texture of coupling,

birth of a wish
      we keep silent
for fear it will dissolve
      a riddle wielding terrible
truth? Nothing gleams more than
      honesty: his trembling hands

speak more about loss than of joy, clumsy
      against my body as he edges
to the opposite end
      of the bed. Boxed inside
the window frame, the faceless
      fan splays light formerly the moon's

bewildered eye.
      Dust flurries, as if first snow of winter,
disseminate from blades—
      a premonition: shadow
against light: a cloud,
      gradation of darkness

shepherding us to
      what we breathe of ourselves:
the promise of exile
      in the inaugurated dawn—

Insomnia

I almost can't see
the possum's poor body
outdoors in the dim night light resting
tall against the trash bin,
her babies nestled in her pouch
like a chamber orchestra of faint
chirruping mouths
clamped around her teats, suckling her to frailty.
I toss her whatever scraps of midnight
snacks I've piled on a plate
then back away.
Her bites barely register a note,
sotto voce,
her paws gently pushing the food into her mouth,
grazioso.
When she is done, she ambles away with her brood
into the crawl space. I hear her dragging herself
through the guts of the house &
follow her gradual processional
to the bathroom
where I flick on the lights,
slide the curtains back & forth,
back & forth across the rod, metal rings screaming
dissonant as violins trembling
each note—C# B A# G—at once, & then her claws
jangle the pipes so that
we make such terrible music this night
& for a while,
each thereafter.

Ennui

Knoxville, Tennessee

A secretary riding the late-night Magnolia sings
her 40-Acres-&-a-Mule song.
Some nights she drowses or dozes off to sleep completely,

the bus rattling down Gay Street to Summit Hill
to Broadway, turning toward her neighborhood
of potholes & teenagers playing chicken

in the middle of the road. Some nights she sings the latest blows
she's been dealt: minimum wage paychecks too small to buy
a new alternator for the car; rent increase on the duplex

& no money to hire someone handy to re-caulk the bathtub,
re-support the sagging roof, return the baby possum
found in the kitchen to its mother.

Her food stamp card reads a low balance,
barely any food left in the cabinets & what's in the freezer
is freezer-burnt, though she'll eat it—she has no choice.

She'll dust the ice crystals off the way she dusts off anything,
eat with a solemn determination, feed the children & bathe them,
whisk them off to bed without a story because she's worked all day

at a living she'll die before ever quitting. So she rides the bus
to save for Christmases & birthdays & the Fourth of July
so her children will know at least minor joy. She rises

in the morning to pour cereal or boil water for oatmeal,
for the briefest breakfast around the family table
because that's what her children want.

It's better than being sent off early to school
for a meal someone else pays for; someone else
who's afforded the luxury of real butter, bacon perfectly crisp,

syrup glistening brown in sunlight filtering through
the white-washed kitchen, across floors of marble stone &
stainless steel appliances wedged between cherry wood cupboards

& Lazy Susans. Who'd begrudge a secretary who wants a home
of vase-filled perennials fragrant with bright blossoms & staunch stems,
a dishwashing machine that doesn't even whisper?

& what a god-send to own liquor cabinets of single malts
& temperature-controlled cruvinets? By the smile on her face,
could this be what she dreams about on a crowded bus,

holding on to the rail because no one believes in affection
for the weary on the Magnolia? With any hope, she won't
arrive home needing to iron the children's school clothes

or scrub the bathtub or call animal control to catch the possum
she finds has returned trapped in the corner behind the stove.
She'd rather sip cheap vodka to make her

forget she works a double the next day with no time in-between shifts
to grab a $5-dollar footlong at Subway or catch an episode
of *The Young & the Restless*. No wonder her head nods

with the constant beat of *tick-tock tick-tock tick-tock*.
She prays to have the energy of several people
living inside her body, ample time to lean against her mop,

a reprieve from domestic work, from the typing pool
where she dreams a life where it's possible to buy
a more opulent toilet each time someone takes a shit

that stains the porcelain, as this means she'll no longer have to
ride the bus, witness another woman standing in the exit
to take a piss or endure a man with Tourette's

sitting next to her because he insists on it,
because he doesn't understand how this disturbs her
from the first chance she's had to sleep all day.

On the Bus
for Kasim

Riding from Knoxville to the Appalachian forests,
I'm hunched in the corner of my seat,
next to a man who seems to be unraveling,
striving for composure in the way
despondent men do: mouth agape
& drooling, eyes sunken as if his face
intends to make a cave of its own flesh.
He moans like there's some creation
struggling to be born, as if
he is reincarnating himself,
as if doing so will allow him a second
chance to avoid mistakes he made
in his past life. & I cannot help but feel
pity for him, as I recall another bus ride,
the number 10 that wound its way around
the heart of Knoxville, & you were there beside me,
breathing softly, I remember, so softly I felt
the machinery of the inner ears churning
to process the sounds you were making.
I asked *what's the matter*, & you hesitated.
So I persisted in the same way I did
when I urged you to make the long, cold walk
from your apartment to mine, to tell you
I tested negative when you were not
in the mood to celebrate as I had, only hours earlier,
with champagne & a lobster tail. & recalling
that moment, I realized why your breath
seemed to whisper. So I wept. Embarrassed.
Which coaxed more tears as I tried to learn compassion.
You said the virus had not taken its toll.
I was relieved. Or was it our years of friendship
that made me unafraid to touch,
to wrap my arms around,
to shoulder your grief?
But where is that compassion now?
This man is resting his bleached head on my shoulder.
For a moment I think it's yours.
But he mumbles about forsythia, four-leaf clovers.
& I'm frightened because I will love you
with the same passion that I wonder if anyone will clamor
to pay respects to this half-living man.

I push him against the window.
Scoot farther to the edge of my seat, shuddering
when I hear his head
knocking against a pane of glass.

HIV Blues

Read me a poem about loss I say.
Are you on the mend? I say.

I shake my head *no.*
I need a poem to ease my anxiety I say.

Why are you anxious I say.
I've lost the compilation of all my favorite sad songs I say.

Have you ever tried listening to opera in foreign languages I say.
All opera is in foreign languages I say.

No, all good *opera is in foreign languages* I say.
But not to those who understand opera I say.

You mean those born in the country of the language I say.
*No, those who understand out of the greatest miseries survive
       the greatest beauty* I say.

You mean the music and the singing I say.
I mean everything I say.

Prayer

Insatiable death come sweetly
as a kiss if you are wise—this is
how I respond to cold embraces.
Ravage me like a lover gone away
so long he's forgotten how my skin
tenses against his. He'll desire me
like orgasm, a small tease of pleasure
that subsides. Make the taking brief—
or let it linger on, the last ember still
glowing long after the fire has died.

Inheritance

Tonight my father drinks alone in his apartment in the projects,
& I in the house I share with my mother. Together, we are
synchronized in the same reams of moonlight
strewn through the trees, these pale white strips unraveling
through the branches. This is how hard liquor tricks the mind
when light flings shadows against our walls—we mistake them
for strangers we pass on the street each day. My father & I speak
across a dark crevasse where he sits folded in the corner
of a room, & I splayed across the bed, each of us with a bottle
dangling by the neck from a poor grip. Whatever we say is spoken
in a slurred, interminable language. Like squawking birds
or turf wars among alley cats. This language fogs the mirrors
we stare into when we realize our unmistakable likeness,
down to the muddied, red-rimmed eyes trapped in our faces.

Existing in the MRI machine after a seizure due to delirium tremens

is like deplaning in a slow single file
conveyer belt of sluggish passengers still wired
into their sleep modes since it's four in the morning
everyone shifting through the narrow aisle
gathering their wits their luggage but not
the human decency to maneuver with purpose
as Houdini once did to escape a straightjacket
padlocked inside a great tank of water
but turtling along as if shackled in ankle-cuffs
chains around their waists connecting more chains
in cross-sections of heavy metallic links
the length of their bodies
escorted on either side by guards
trundling in their own lackadaisical fashion
securing these passengers-turned-captives
beneath the arms & down the long corridor
they schlepp to the execution chamber
shuffling while meantime your head aches in peril
the kind of pain that must be like a blown-out tire
& no spare & the driver wracking his head
against the steering wheel until he groans
with regret for not spending a little extra
for a measly donut & now he's stranded on the side of the road
with passersby carrying on the usual business of apathy
or else there isn't enough time to stop & offer assistance
as they are needed at the airport to collect their friends & relatives
whisk them home unaware they're in no hurry so early
in the morning to be "collected" weary as they are
as it's been from Seattle to Portland to Atlanta to Knoxville
one insufferable layover & no booze to keep you starry-eyed
like a child's propitious discovery of the well-kept secret
hideaway where the candy is kept
& he'll sort through all the options of how
to make his belly ache as you would indulging a liquor
cabinet's inventory to reacquaint yourself with a reliquary of spirits
you've been long without but still
jubilant as though you've happened upon
the most desirable of sundries
no more collateral damage
of days ransacking a room for even a milliliter
titled into the bottom of an errant bottle &
later crawling the floor with a lampshade around your ankles

purring like a walrus
all of this a sign of the wretched past & presently
a celebration akin to the serendipitous unearthing
of a chest of jewels buried among the ruins of a derelict field
if only the drink that brings back your soul will assuage this aching
that refers itself throughout your body
the way a clot transfers itself from the leg to the left ventricle
if it wants to kill a man if it wants
to commit itself to healing
the suffering you endure
when there isn't a swill of liquor to be had
when a kink in the machinery reduces you to shivers
if you don't soon taste the elixir to calm
your beating heart coding the S.O.S.
as you slope toward the revelation
you're inside the belly of a ravenous beast

Delirium Tremens

It's the body's yearning to be sober. The first
bead of sweat forming at the temple. It's

subtle tremors in the limbs, a forewarning quake
even the animals sense & hence the stampede.

It's lying restless the way electrocution
makes one restless. & hair of the dog won't subdue.

It's covering the mouth when the volume's turned to
shrill in the third circle of hell. It's gluttony's

flame engulfing the skin like parchment one's sin is
writ upon. It's light splintering behind the eyes.

It's fever's encroachment. It's phosphene trickery,
prisoner's cinema in a blacked-out room, &

not a sliver of fluorescence. It's cowering
beneath sheets praying to god. It's the absence of

god. It's the lion's share of disasters. A tree
fallen across live wires, magnificent sparks that

burn a village to the ground. It's everything
that aspires to flickers. It's imagining these

catastrophes. Citizens woebegone for the
sake of their homes, burnt-edge leaves scattering the ground.

It's everyone fallen to their knees raking
their past into charred hands, sorting through all the old

feelings that made them happy at last. It's no more
to show for it. It's "this never happened." Body's

betrayal enlisting a mind not intact.
It's slowly breaking down, cauterized from years of

chronic drinking & pill-popping toppling one's
resolve when the bottle's empty. It's shrinking to

corners when hallucinogens pull shadows from
the walls like demon hieroglyphs come alive. It's

marionettes with severed strings, delirium
tremens through the flesh all the way through to the toes

curled in anguish. It's bones cracking under the weight
of pain. The inability to distinguish

one fiery pulse from another. It's howling all
the same. It's crawling the bed. It's a wrecking crew's

steel ball swinging. It's disassembling one from
the inside out & no doubt about suffering.

It's the ravishing one must endure. It's healing.

Auguries: A Love Story

I have a drinking problem
that requires hospitalization.

Congestive heart failure
the cardiologist says,

proceeding with so many
questions he seems

more interested in the facts
than what to do with them.

Doctor of infectious
diseases arrives three days later

with more news:
positive for HIV. Within hours,

my love enters the room
sipping a Solo cup of beer,

sits next to my bed while Mama & Daddy
stand vigil, all of us

carrying on about change,
about fear. I know

he isn't just pretending to listen
when he tells me to shut up & rest.

The next day he forces me
to eat my dinner.

On another, he shrugs
off work

when plans are made to
snake a catheter into my heart.

He pleads for everyone
to pray for me, for the doctor

performing my "surgery,"
which is wrong.

It's only a "procedure"
that brings an entire community

to its knees
with needless worry.

I leave the hospital with a life
vest that resembles a sports bra.

He asks me to lie with him
along his chest

on the sofa as he fingers
my ears. Yes,

he can be tender
as I try to be comfortable

despite the heart-
monitoring sensors pressing

into my flesh to save my life
as though sweetening the pot

when my position allows me to be
the little spoon as we

fall asleep with his arm
tight around my torso, his hand

latticing my hand, his face
breathing in the nape of my neck

imploring god's mercy
upon me. He weeps so quietly

I never would've known
despite such pathos,

he is planning to dump me,
when I should've known the signs

were disguised as endorphins
leaving my body in an easy composure.

Though I can survive
a heart in ruin, long as it still beats,

even when, eventually,
I'll need to return the key

to his house. It has passed
through many hands with many names

to correspond to its many purposes:
"spare" key;

"emergency pit stop/I need
a place to smoke weed"

key; "just in case you leave
something behind" key...

all the ellipses meaning it's
anyone's guess to whom

it might be given next.
I knew it'd be me

anticipating the prospect
the way a pageant girl is assured

she's the winner
when the runner-up stands aside

allowing Pageant Queen emerita
to place the shimmering crown

upon her head.
I paraded the room waving

a hand demure as if
the marquee act *du jour*.

I told my friends about it.
I told my family about it.

I went to church
to worship

about it. The choir sang
about it. Preacher preached

about it. Had I the resources,
I would have advertised it

on the front page
of the *News Sentinel.*

One unequivocal headline:
"DARIUS GOT THE KEY."

But now:
the Pageant Queen's reign: *fini!*

What does it mean:
return the key so he, in turn,

gives it to the-new-
someone-else.

Do I consider myself
one of the many blips

I've mistaken for stars
short circuiting the sky?

He no longer loves me—
yes:

retaliate, ceremoniously:
tell him *I no longer love you,*

an emphatic lie
like mailing him

a card homemade,
picture of a man fishing from a boat

on a lake reluctant to shimmer
as it should, water appearing, instead,

as if black slate of granite
the sun will never reflect...

It's only a key
given me in case I forgot

my messenger bag
(whatever)

when I left any number of mornings
during the trial period

obviously lasting long enough
to test my *joie de vie.*

So, in the interest of full disclosure:
alert the press

so everyone knows: Darius has a key.
Explain:

it isn't "you're the love of my life,
here's the key to my house"

key. No. It's
"another winter has passed

& we didn't last a year...
not even"

key.

My father walks in rain with no umbrella

from his apartment in the projects
to the liquor store a few blocks away,

deeper in the projects. People ask why he's
walking in rain with no umbrella. He explains
it's one of few ways he's brought closer to god.

They don't understand he means
rain will make his hair grow.
He wants a larger Afro. He's faithfully

divine when he's vodka-drunk—
that's to say gin-drunk without juniper berries.
When he's rain-soaked he's scoffed at,

the cultural milieu of the projects having shifted
the years since he became this man
haggard in clothes clinging wet

to his frail frame, how so much idle time & fifths
of Kamkatcha have rendered his skin & bones
to skin & bones. This is why we call it *Gonegetcha.*

My father walks in rain with no umbrella to
prove he doesn't need to wear flashy suits
as he did in his youth, before rap moguls

made them fashionable, before Steve Harvey
& his double-breasted successes made buttons
the new business bling, apropos for showmanship.

A seizure causes my father to split a gash so deep
in his tongue he speaks with a clenched jaw, a pronounced limp
as if referred pain from his mouth has handicapped his leg.

When he walks in rain with no umbrella he walks, too,
without a make-shift cane, as when he misses my mother
& can hardly stand to walk at all.

He doesn't tell me this, only I see it in his face
fatigued as he chews his bottom lip, as his tongue,
swelled to the size of a small boat docked

between his teeth, allows words—
wife, divorce, fault—to form as if lottery balls
appearing as random utterances from his lips.

My father's lonely as a man who loses the lottery.
I tell him there's always next time.
He asks for five dollars to get himself a bottle.

All I've got are quarters I pour into his hands.
He's glad for it & hugs my neck tight—
as if the band around an umbrella,

as if he's just hit the jackpot.

My Mother's Hands

For some time I'd known
my father's knuckle prints

in the cement wall painted over.
My mother's lip purpling,

a touch of pink
where the underflesh

bloomed
through the bruise.

I wasn't so young
I couldn't reason. & so

wondered how long the scars
would last. Not those of her face.

But the daily routines she continued,
saying nothing while she

opened mail with the blade
of her index finger, loaded

laundry, detergent unrinseable
beneath hard water of the kitchen

sink, a permanent stain
her hands felt even as she smoothed

wrinkles away from my pants,
before the hot steam of an iron,

& skeptical
whether she was getting it

just right. Her hands were
meant for grounding

onions & bell peppers
into meat for a loaf,

for gliding a glass up
a patient's chin, slaking off

drool running
from his lip,

but mostly for holding
my face after a week-long

trip to camp, a gesture
so beneficent

she should one day have them
appraised. These

were my mother's hands, that
even curled into a fist would not

fit the indentations
in a wall

she scrubbed
until paint chipped away,

the brick sunken like a tiny cave
a face makes of itself

from malnourishment,
or a sickness that withers flesh

from bone—
a blueprint of a body that,

when I see it, I consider
how it all happened—

by which, I mean, her touch,
& how, after all these years,

it feels amputated,
& memory unable to mend

what the mind has unstitched.
I might one day come to understand

a mind forgets
what it doesn't want to remember—

like my father's hands searing
a day

into my mother's face.
How she shielded herself

with hands a latticework so tight
no light could enter through.

In the Clair de Lune

At the end of this pale, phosphorescent day,
a curtain of black birds swoop-flutters & parts, revealing
two beautiful men. Nothing more than gauze, filaments
of cloud rolling at the silver rim. Rippled limbs
entangle like knots of vine on trees as one
lover fists the arced moon, an ornament gliding down
his arm. At the bank's edge, I dress down to bare
flesh, waiting for the scythe of moon to appear undulant
on the surface. I'll splash into stars, swim
stroke by stroke through chilling membrane,
determined to wade, ecstatic, in its nook.

Self-Portrait as Recurring Bird

On any day
when a bird

appears
a mistake

in my noon
tea, I stir it

with my silver
spoon, fish

out feathers
floating

on the surface,
so surprised

the bird ripples,
reforms

whole, so
unfettered

by clink-
clatter

silver insists
upon porcelain

as I
swirl round

& round, bird
after endless

bird chasing
its tail-feathers,

which becomes
a man

spinning
like a top

on the black
face of the sea.

I know this
man as I've known

nights marred
by dawn's

residuals—as in
moon-glow

unrevealed
when day holds

deep in its
pockets, light,

where gods weep
through tears

of laughter
at my misfortunes

because I want
what's been

tarnished, tug
memory

like wind
escorting

wayward birds
to their boughs.

It's fragility
that beckons

the past,
as I reside in

a vicious house
of ghosts

haunting me
to erasure,

like cataracts
stitching shut

the eyes,
where blankness

forces memory
to substitute

what becomes
lost in the actual

world: window
panes streaming

with overdue
rains, eaves

rattling, birds
tuck-beaked

in their nests—
whose songs

become rapture.
Grieving, yes,

is an option,
though so is

desiring
contentment—

like a bird's ruby eye
flickering

a kind
of wonderment

I find
when realizing

a long-earned
dream. It's as if

the silver edge
of heaven

has incubated
in the central

nervous system,
& each day

it glimmers
is another day

waking without
sobbing &

regretting
what the cosmos

has made
unrequited:

each hour
another

recompense,
each hour

a songbird
rehearsing

its nocturnal
overture,

wing-bent
& relishing

the promise of
an abiding night.

Epithalamion

Dear brother, here I am.
Outside. Evening's descended
upon a pocket of light
I crouch in—
so tainted
compared to the brilliance
that surrounds you: women
glittering in beaded dresses, waiters
with champagne flutes tinkling
at their rims, orbiting
around you. Mouths gleam
with toothy grins
caught in camera light
flashes. & brightest
of them all are men
with tie clips—gold & silver—flickering
like heat lightning of insects
buzzing among the brambles,
in the ivy & kudzu.

~

In moments there will be a toast.
Your new wife will join you
at your side; confetti will be thrown,
& this will be rapture,
just as, years from now,
you will cherish your children—
whose laughter will fill the house
when their mother, your wife, scoops them
into her arms & presses them
to her heart as though such innocence
can be contained in a simple moment
of delight. Or more like the summers
when you all will visit the quarry,
wade knee-deep in the cool licks,
& afterward sun yourselves
on the bank, listening
to the water ebb, & this sound
will become a moment that will burst
inside each of you
each time rain sops the earth,

becomes drizzle, & you savor
the pungent smell the earth gives up
after a hard rain.

~

I'm here, my brother,
still. A moth's papier mâché wings
trapped between the slats
of the blinds, nothing but a faceless
specter ruined the way a heart is
ruined when our mother weeps
into her hands, refusing to tremble
even a smile, or our father knocking back vodka
one after the other, his crossed leg
shaking so hard it would crack
at the joint when either of them sights
two men circled by friends, toasting
their nuptials.

~

Dear brother, I was there
to endure the silence
when our mother & father left
defeated. She retreated into the wings
of her body, & he unable to hold
his head up high in the custom
he was taught as a boy—
& that was the memory that lasted,
though yours, I'm sure will be much more
celebrated: a roomful haloing you,
your bride, with praise,
& the picture frames already
purchased & positioned on the mantels
in the houses of your beloveds, my own
frames lying face down,
the stand lifted from the back
like the marker of a grave.

~

Part II

~

Sotto Voce

In the apartment above us,
our neighbor plays the violin

horribly. Baroque music by the sound of it,
but I can't be sure. I want to ask,

but you're fast asleep, or at least pretending
to be. A light breeze through the curtains

strings the noise into our room
& I can almost forgive it, but I have to

contend with the snore caught in your throat,
which I suppose is your subtle way of saying

a duet with this indelicate
violinist is better than a conversation

with me. It's always been this way
between the two of us, mimicking

the frailties of a couple
who has nothing more in common

than a fox has
to its prey. You were always

so cunning. You'd have to be
to pretend this music is tender.

Are you dreaming of our neighbor?
The sadness in his face as he plays?

How a clink in the body's machinery
has forced a migration of his senses?

Is our neighbor at the window
shivering the way this music trembles

every nerve in my body
with ingratitude? He seems

to gesture with his bow for you
to join him, your snores softer

as the music becomes more intolerable.
This is how I know tonight

you've left me forever. Though I will
feel fine in the morning, will not

throw fits. I will feed upon this
knowing as if it were a sacrament.

Though there will be
a sadness you must understand

will never return me wholly as I was
before. If you listen, you can hear

the music blessing me with a gradual
diminuendo. It's almost bearable now.

So I will sleep now, next to you, enduring
as best I can the quiet

of your sleep. Hope if I can suffer
my way next to your body

I can withstand this breeze sifting in,
this dull ache in my bones.

Statues in the Park

Toward the end of day & wishing
again for daylight. What's discernible is

evening's impending gloom. If we'd admit it,
this is a sad occasion:

us perched at separate ends of a park bench;
block-headed statues in the dark looming

behind us holding so dearly to one another.
This is what makes art. What art makes of us:

models for statues battling stubbornness.
We try to one-up the other without too much effort,

since that would lessen the impact
of the plan. Which would be what, exactly?

To wax sullen in the afterglow of day gone awry
is to hold our tongues as best as we can.

As for these statues, they bear no resemblance
to any human frailty; though their actions speak

as much about truth as any whose skulls are shaped
to resemble childish drawings of perfect squares.

Perhaps this suggests there is kindness
in our obstinacy—each of us somehow regarding the gift

of winning as if it were the daily courier
arriving with news the earth is no longer a viable place

to live. An absurdity, yes; though a game two men can play—
holding & holding on, as if forever, to silence,

fearing what becomes a man who
clings only to what's left standing.

Aubade

Dearest, we've become merely
the taste of our salt-licked bodies.
Bent at the alter in daylight—
twilight beckoning. We feel blessed
to endure. We are succor
& no way out the maze.
Coupling even now will not
bear us chambered in flat notes,
cordoned off from music.
Mi amour, the kiss holds our tongues.
We would sing if only our mouths would.

Myopia
for Robert Sanchez

All day I find long, black hairs
in the washing machine, coiled

around the oven knobs, in the mustard

of my sausages & kraut...
I think to whom might they belong—

someone I've loved (or obsessed over,

confusing it for love), or someone I've known
casually, had met him at a party, gazing

over a keg; perhaps between the aisles in a supermarket;

in the dim flickers of light at the Cineplex.
I need to know so I search through photo albums,

pile them on the floor, one after the other, holding

the strands against black-cropped heads, using
a magnifying glass for closer comparison, but no luck.

I open a phone book, dial numbers, names

A-Z—describe the hairs, entangle them,
describe the helixes, the knots & shadows—

how each strand thickens & thins

like a snake's tail only in the softest light.
Who has hair like that? No one knows.

I'm in fits of frustration. People call me crazy,

even at the haberdashery as I sort through piles
& piles of hats, attaching strands inside the brim, picturing

how *his* hair might flow from there

like a shadow against the forehead.
I run to the store-keep, eyes blood-shot, panting

& sweating & ask him for names, clues, but receive

only a blank stare, as if I've fabricated the whole thing—
as if there's a chance the hairs are merely the light

catching a scratch in the machine, on the oven...

I leave the shop lion-muscled, but not of heart—
for grief pitches stones against my heart

as if it were an abandoned house.

I return home, to the sites of the hairs, but
they're gone now, & I can't help but feel

like a man who's lost his lover after a long illness

& must endure the uninterrupted
goings-on of life the way a man who lies in bed

feels warmth dissipating from an empty space

where a lover has never slept,
a lover who was never even there.

Even Bones

Don't tell me the tongue's
Not a magical place.

—Clare Rossini

You can't deny a tongue knows the magical
places a body tenders on those garrulous nights
when too many vodkas on the rocks loosen the muscle,
secrets unraveling more like proffering too much
information about the balloon-knot pucker between
the legs—it's a celebration, like realizing
one can perform pirouettes in sensible shoes,
though we prefer the spangled ones, but we take
what we can get, are delighted when one inspired
move turns anodyne to sublime: a thread-through-needle-eye
precision of a tongue navigating various routes
of an insatiable body—those unknown places
where even bones quiver the way a river slicks
then swallows whole all the various stones.

The "Keep It on the Down Low" Rhythm & Blues Show

R's breath against B's
neck suggests R fucks
to *rock the boat.*
But—spoiler alert—
R has a fiancée
at home piling
dishes in a dirty sink
from a day's-worth
cooking recipes
R wants to eat
to reminisce dining
al fresco some city
in Italy where waiters
with lithe hands wafted
exotic aromas his
way. He adored
firm asses, preferred
pronouns
he, him, his,
on the sly,
not so much
pigeons who
cooed & shit the
cobbled pathways.
No homo
did nothing
in the end
to dissuade
R's appetite.
In fact, it encouraged
fiancée's labor
to ply him with
those familiar
tastes & smells,
persuade R's eyes
to the left, to the left
inside his head,
a manner such as
during sex or for love
of good food—she
knows R's moods,
how to make him

swoon even when
his hard-on is
for B & means
bend over
let me see you
shake a tail feather.
Meanwhile wife-to-be's
home wringing
her hands & R's
grinding his hips
I want to rock with you
because, yes, this
trifling ass,
—low down—
"down low" shit
is still going on,
so it's best
to keep it still
hush hush
when B relents
since R
tempts the flick
of his tongue
between whispers—
how do you want it?
B's drawers can't slip
to his feet
quick enough,
feel the heartbeat
pulse
behind
his knees,
weakened when he
grabs ankles, arches
his back & begs R to just
give it to me, baby.

Self-Portrait as Uncle on the Down Low

My niece hears the ice cream truck & begs *Uncle*.
I fear she wants to know why I'm childless, why I've

provided no cousins, no grandchildren for my
mother & father. She asks again & the noose

tightens. The gulp I swallow lodges above the
knot. *Would you like to help load the dishwasher?* I

ask. But she isn't satisfied. *Uncle,* she says
though there's no question, no statement discernible

in her voice. She taps a bony finger against
her lip as if she knows a secret. *Uncle,* she says

as though it's my preternatural station
in life—the way a bridesmaid is always a bride's

maid; the way single men with male companions are
both called uncle when the families gather for

Sunday dinners or reunions. She looks at me
with *Dora the Explorer* eyes. *Uncle,* she says

her voice scaling toward the upper register
of the staff, an apparent question, though one it

seems she already knows the answer to: *never
end sentences in prepositions… or is it*

with *prepositions,* I tell her. She studies me
as if she's the Encyclopedia Brown for

the Justin Bieber generation. *Uncle,* she
says without ever following through, suggesting

I know where this is going, the accusation
dividing the syllables into equal parts. I

think back to when she was an infant I held just
moments after her birth, how she startled so

suddenly in my shaking arms, flushed against my
chest, my fingers having slightly unhinged she must

have felt certain of slipping through the split & each
mother present in that room reached, demanded I

hand over the child. Even then she incited
fear. *Uncle* is all she'll say, & what else do I

do except cup her chin in my palm, draw her gaze
away. I'm not married. No girlfriend. *Uncle*, she says

until the room we're in is a gallery
of journalists & paparazzi, a judge poised

to swing the gavel, a jury scrutinizing my
every movement from the box: what are my hands

doing? have my eyebrows lifted too far? too arched?
Uncle, she repeats until the bodies in this

newly formed room lean forward in their seats, witness
Mt. Vesuvius in a sundress destroying

Pompeii. *Uncle*, she says as if testing whether
I can extend the months since my last drink, how I'm

tempted to pour a shot of rum from underneath
the kitchen sink. *Uncle*. Chase it with beer. *Uncle*.

Fill my head with cumuli, a soft rain that falls
like spring water over stones. *Uncle*. I just might

risk sobriety for the chance it'll silence
her tongue. *Uncle*, she says & nothing else. *Uncle*,

she says as when she wants a jelly sandwich or
grilled cheese, to bounce on the neighbor's trampoline in

the back yard. *Uncle*, she says nodding her head to
the sound of *row row row your boat* blaring from the

ice cream truck's bullhorn for all these many *uncles*.
I pull a five from my pocket & she takes it

swiftly out the door. I won't see her again
until evening, when I must call her in, when

half-inside the house she pleads to stay outdoors while
there's still a phosphorescent glow of daylight left.

Poem to a Son

Finally I'm trying to forget
the impossibility I will ever father

a son.
Then remembering I'm trying

to forget, I remember
the forgetting & am heartbroken,

lying in bed, twilight slicing
horizontal lines

into my flesh,
as if the arced moon intends to remind me

I'm prisoner to a grave fault.
& if the stretch of night would give itself

over to my grief, I would wrench
the crescent—stardust, helixes of galaxies,

isotopes, invisible matter—
from its smug, overbearing suspension.

But how will I feel in the morning, when
I overhear the old couple next door arguing

because the perfume of her gladiolas has become
so overwhelming, & he complains

of allergies? But later they make up
as there's something to be said

about the long-coupled. They remind me
we must find shameless happiness

wherever it may be—in woodpiles
they spend stacking together, preparing

for winter. In the screech
of a raccoon chasing ghosts up cedars.

Even in the old house of my boyhood,
where the neighbors have a son.

A boy
I've seen only in the dim corner of his room,

back against window, tucked playing.
Some nights I've watched him

as his father stoops over the hill of his back,
gliding hands along the ridges of spine.

I watch the child lean into the cupped palm,
his father scratching the fine hairs of his head,

& I imagine joy welling inside a boy
with a face like mine.

Self-Portrait Approaching Thirty

When I see them bouncing their basketballs,
catching them beneath their shirts, it's like magic—
future Hall-of-Famers right here
in my own backyard. I'm not so athletic
because I drink too much &
my shirt hugs me like a jilted lover who can't let go
of the past. There are days, though, when I wish I could
pass a ball between my legs without injury,
but I'm better at mixing drinks, letting loose spirits
in the house. Sometimes when I smoke
I imagine my bank account's as full as my lungs
& then, perhaps, I could afford lessons,
show these boys how to shoot a ball
through a hoop of smoke. Now that's a trick.
They might shake my hand because they have to
show respect but will talk smack to their friends
behind my back. What they might say
can be summed up in a phrase:
I'm a drunk. No trickster
but an illusionist to convince them
if not for me they'd be hitching dogs to Radio Flyer wagons.
(Though I may have had a shot of vodka too much
if I believe that.) I recall a dream in which I'm holding
in my hands a loved one's ashes, a charred departed life
left to my charge, & I awake with such a start my head knocks
against a light fixture I hadn't known was there & then
I realize I've been pushed closer
to the end of the line. Closer, even, than these boys
who, tonight, will roll their socks
into balls, toss them into clothes hampers,
making with their mouths the noise of a crowd gone wild,
& consider themselves men,
which allows them to sleep more soundly.
They'll one day buy palatial mansions for their mamas
& drive Humvees because their lives have come to this,
the reason bravura must prevail
if they are to become magicians on stilts
& date the prettiest girls who will bear them
children with eyes gleaming in the stars.

A Tryst

I tried to be a gigolo once, but
neither of us knew why

I thought I'd ever be good at it.

I almost made a castrato of him
when I went down on him,

because it was my first time.

We passed each other
beneath barely luminous light

& I knew he'd think I'd be spectacular—

how we circled each other like secrets
circulating amongst people who refuse the truth,

needing, instead, to make up fictions.

I've never blamed him
for sitting next to me grimaced &

slump-shouldered in a motel

in the well-lit savage part of the city
listening to a couple behind paper-

thin walls fucking the way strangers do—

nothing but limbs hyphenating other limbs,
hands palming pelvises, bodies flickering

in spotlight of cars passing by their window,

their muted screeches like traffic
of alley cats—

I wanted to fuck him then & there

just thinking about it. & I tried,
& I smiled at him, but he turned away

refusing even a glimpse of me,

& I'd never felt so unconsidered,
as if I were a bench on which he could rest

his disregard, that this was a mistake

to think we could be anything more
than passing acquaintances.

I waited in silence until he fell asleep—

the room being paid for through the night—
& listened to him make a noise like a walrus's

skin sliding into the muck of wet sand,

slowly circling deeper into delirium,
like his sleep, but not like sleep. Like death.

I imagined his body slowly decomposing,

each chest fall & rise another second
ticked off his life. I whispered to him,

are you dying, leaving me,

as if we were lovers. But he was silent
despite his noise, & I confused by how much

I admired his tranquility, how he shone

in the moon's light casing his skin,
the bones of that room.

I wanted to sidle up against his body,

find comfort in his stillness. I wanted to
pull him closer to visit his body a while,

the way long-time companions hold each other

in a swallow of light & think nothing
of the silence, how the absence of sound

compels one to find comfort in the simplest gestures.

We were strangers meeting for a quick fuck
that never happened. & I was no gigolo—

though it was a small price to pay

simply to be beside him,
waiting out the night.

Communally Bound

In the early Sunday morning drowse
of the Travis County Jail, we are

paired off, handcuffed,
each to another & shuffling

in our over-sized flip-flops,
make our way to court, waiting

for a judge to appear in his choir robe,
yawning & wringing his eyes of sleep

between reading, one by one, the charges
we each face. I am handcuffed to a man

who is light-skinned—redbone we'd call him
in the ghetto—who insists on scratching

his balls each time the judge pauses
to allow Spanish translators to repeat

charges the non-English speaking are
facing, whether or not the court should

contact the Mexican consulate, & so forth,
& it seems this man has made a game of this—

at once enticing & irritating—like so many men
I've met outside these court room walls,

& he might as well be any one of them, except
the tattooed tear below his right eye suggests

he is not one given to sentimentality—
a perpetual crier—but he is a murderer—

yes, that is what the tear means—&
I wonder what circumstances brought him

to such depths of human frailty—to kill
a man & have forever stamped on his face

the night it all went down—a drive-by shooting,
a knife wedged between someone's heart

& lungs somewhere in a black alley, the possibilities
are endless—& I shake my head, chuckle,

knowing the crimes he's committed far supersede
the drunk-driving charges he is now facing,

& no one is the wiser save those who can read symbols
on a man's face & know he has completed

a rite of passage, a Bar Mitzvah of the ghetto
variety, though how does my second-degree

felony charge stack against his crimes, I wonder—
me, who prefers Pinot Gris to malt liquor, me

who sautés & brines, writes the moon into a story
of unrequited love, me who witnesses

tufts of pubic hair wiring their way upward
each time he scratches himself, pondering

if it could ever work out between us.
Or is it the bond of incarceration

that binds us as we are wrist-bound
to one another, as if we are indeed

a portrait of perfect compatibility
—his Eliza Doolittle to my Prof. Higgins.

Though of course, this is mere fantasy,
synapses snapped in the brain preventing

mind's access to rational thought—
though in bearing this, seeds of regret blossom

in my throat & I am choked with grief, knowing
this is the end of our courtship, & I must touch

everywhere but where our wrists are
communally bound, kiss his lips,

that lone tear, awaken him from a life
that has led him to this place.

Dawn

approaches like fingers finessing keys
of a baby grand

inside a pit of grief. Music,
a tragedy waging against the body—

like dahlias unfolding petals
in search of light

but failing to enter into that brightness.
The body wounds. The heart

orders no affection for familiar kindness
as if this is the way to make sense

of the strangeness that is the world,
as if the world is the climax

& the orchestra enters
a fraction behind the beat.

Intimacies in Borrowed Light

I've chosen a quiet place in this great old house,
wandered the rooms, gazed out the windows:
Spanish moss tangled like silly string
in the cypress, great mounds of it floating
in a pool where a couple may have taken a midnight
swim, brushed the strands from their arms, maybe
mistook them for exposed veins—fibrous, infected,
relentlessly inescapable. This is where my imagination turns
whimsical to glum, I know, though I can't help but to wonder
if this empty house signals the end of their love,
if the signs were in a sky pockmarked with stars,
as though the cosmos had unleashed its grief
upon the world: Spanish moss & stars: the signs?
No... forgive me. It may be the silence is too ingratiating.
I've forgotten what it feels like to curl one's body
into the curl of another & wait out the night
in cathedral silence, just a kiss or two at the nape
of the neck for assurances, because, after all,
this moment is one of the great palaces of the world:
intimacies in borrowed light of a moon or lamp-like glow
of a hundred fireflies just outside your window, you listening
to wave after wave of latticed sounds filling each room
with possibilities of surviving the night, & waking
the next day eager for the hours to peel away
until you reach the hour when everything repeats.

Primer

In bed again listening to the quiet.
It's in the silence where I admit
a broken heart is no more a bruise than ecstasy is

a sign of too much happiness.
It's easier sometimes to untangle knots
with my teeth, my hands fretting.

If a straight line of rope can be
salvaged, there is hope yet. There is a song for this.
I imitate it each time I awaken,

feeling I've sunk so far deep inside
myself it seems I'll never return to normal.
Like now. These stars are not arpeggios in a song.

This is assigning too much meaning. All I ask is
if he can bring himself to say I love you
one last time, let it be in one slow breath.

Troubled Lovers

All night we make love,
he & I, a cautionary tale
for troubled lovers who,

in what we call afterglow,
are blanched in what was once
a beautiful moon, as now it appears dull

& listless as our limbs which,
in the height of passion, found new
routes to exploring rapture, our bodies

akimbo in the spread-out thinness
of the room's ecstasies, the weight
of experience no match for the jaded

cities that erect themselves in the post-
coital hours inhabited by all the others
he & I found fidelity bountifully

available when too much of a good thing
signaled the end of love.
So on it goes, each night, the same

routine: he coming up from behind, or me
an agent of due process washed-out
in limelight of a moon's shuddering

filigrees, lying there as if principal
in my own tragedy, a funereal celebration
in which one after another turns & walks away,

without a backwards glance, without a care
for the sacrifices he & I pretended
would make all the difference.

Leitmotif

Across the way the neighbors again argue
the virtues of fidelity & discretion.
I've come out into the cold, dark winter
the white elephant smoking a cigarette,
leaning against the porch-rail intruding upon
their privacy, such impertinence I feel
like a child disobedient. Without coat
or toboggan, a cup of hot water to warm
their hands, one talks, the other pretends
to see a crack in the sky. Each voice
pitches louder, a constant campaign
of half-truthing, fictioning, then their voices
lowing, their heads craning my direction,
toward the smoke, the spire lifted in my hand
a dying torch & me shrinking back
as if from a scolding hand. Against my lips
a snifter of cognac might betray how clearly
I'm a saboteur of their feuding. A box
of Harry London chocolates poised
for sampling is a veiled attempt at metaphoring
I'm a sweetheart who enjoys a good show—
half-nelsoned as if by a Mahler symphony.
But even Mahler isn't so bullying,
the way the air is now a deeper purple,
night beaten to a plum,
as they each refuse to see inside
the heart of the matter, which is
almost like tossing salt over one's shoulder
to preserve some semblance of luck.
I'd like to tell them that, if only to conform
to the idea of wisdom coming from the mouths
of babes. Because I do have something to say.
Though often, I admit, (when I do say)
I'm the pummeled air between my neighbors
that bars her from tracing a finger along the crease
of his shirt sleeve, or him from blurting out
the biggest shock of all: that he's fallen out of love
& can't continue on this way, & then I have to admit
sometimes words fail, that more & more
words are instruments of futility, like trying
to conceive that pennies fall from heaven,
or when one pulls the beds apart

the other spends the night restless on the couch
because they each possess a god-like wrath,
a stubbornness that keeps a deer stationary
in the wake of oncoming traffic.
My neighbors can't hear themselves out
to hear the imminent crash. They find a sort of peace
from knowing one will walk away with blood
on their hands. That's how they know they've won
& one day will tell their children how
they left the other in a downward spiral, not
able to pick their battered body up off the ground,
& this, they will say, is how to prove resilience,
(or worse) that they're not one to be trifled with.
If you were here you would know all that I say
is true because you, too, have tried to settle in
for the night but are called back again
& again by voices across the way rising
like the resurrection. It becomes news to you
the same way senseless tragedies encourage
pillow-talk or campfire stories, gossip
at the water cooler while the boss is in
the boardroom. You hear this news the same way
you hear a turkey buzzard lifting up heavily
from a tree branch & the leaves hitting the roof
of the car below like drum-taps. You hear it like rain
when there is no rain & you so badly desire it
because you've never seen the earth so parched,
or anything, for that matter, fighting the good fight
to survive & losing so terribly.

Aftermath

We start with trout amandine,
lemon & capers, the insatiable appetite,

& this is when we fall in love
with smells of sauté & bellies swoon—

garlic mashed & smashed potatoes with skins,
mushroom caps butter-sizzled, drizzling

two spoons of balsamic, shallots chop-diced
with pepper & salt just right to taste. Recipe or ode,

we don't know except to relish & swallow,
trapped gape-mouthed in delicious fervor—

forth & back rocking in our chairs,
slapping our knees with flat palms—

it's all so delicious & eventually we settle ourselves
propped-elbows on the dinner table & drink more

from our wine glasses, rub our stomachs until
each morsel situates in every cranny

& we can blow off sleep a while longer,
bear ourselves to gray light of an early evening.

We push the boat out along the river & carry on
the insufferable pathos of two men bored

by life's little disasters, bunker down in a shivering heap,
rain-drenched when storm clouds belly-up

& like that— snap—no more of light's resplendent fracturing
& neither does the river matter to us anymore.

So we paddle to shore, the water chopped up
by oar-stroke, fists of rain. We might huddle

beneath terrycloth, stoke a fire, but it seems enough
tucking our knees, sitting naked back to back

beside a portable heater, opening a window
to the misty rain as if a need to receive

a little something more for ourselves.

Self-Portrait in Atlanta, Georgia
for Torrance
1979-2016

Clouds floating along an imperfect sky
remind me this isn't a dream.

The two of us, silent & weary,
are evidence of a body's slow decomposing.

When he speaks, *there's so much I have to tell you,*
I know what's coming.

Sky blinks with planes taking off & landing.
Tall buildings teeter their bright heads toward Orion's Belt.

I've tested positive, he says.
I feel the ocean roiling inside me.

I hear white noise more & more pervasive
as I ascend a steep mountain

in this empty parking lot we sit in,
beneath a vast strip of what we consider

beauty: the disembodied night,
pale eye half shut, decked in her shawl

of stars, clouds of hair
stretched for miles as if she's lost

all control of her faculties.
He asks, *did you hear me?*

I tell him, *there's a piano solo in the feather
theme to Forrest Gump, right before*

the moaning ghosts begin to sing.
What does that mean? he asks.

I bow my head, trying hard to still my voice.
What else is there to say?

HIV Blues

A man this beautiful and still his lover leaves him I say.
Ah despair! I say.

I would vomit my heart every day I say.
Of all the ways to express maximum sadness I say.

Of course, it's a great human trick I say.
It could get you a spot on Letterman I say.

Letterman's retired I say.
Of all the missed opportunities I say.

To dress in polka-dots and stripes and high-waters and boots with
    fish in the heels I say.
That is disastrously grotesque I say.

I don't believe you take me seriously anymore I say.
Why should I when I'm not a celebrity whoremonger? I say.

Indeed you aren't, and neither have you been a subject for Andy
    Warhol I say.
Nor you maestro of the Boston Pops conducting the New World
    Symphony I say.

But I've been to Rome and experienced its exquisite architecture I say.
And I have been to Vienna and conversed extensively with scholars of
    Beethoven's Moonlight Sonata I say.

But could you recognize the first chord without hearing the 1st
    movement? I say.
Did you pocket a piece of ancient history, a brick to display on the
    mantel? I say.

You will not beach me like a baby whale I say.
But darling the constant ebb and flow will surely cast you back out to
    sea I say.

You sound almost contrite I say.
Because you've run out of pages in the magazine I say.

Do you think we are on the verge of an existential crisis? I say.
I suppose it depends on the tabloids I say.

A Bachelor at 36

I insert *does not* between he & love me—
verify I'm crawling inside
my feelings. When that doesn't work,

I'm petty & dirty the floor with torn petals
to retaliate against a group of my friends
dancing at a wedding I wasn't invited to.

Sometimes what momentarily marks a sense
of sadness may as easily be a sign to call Mama—
her face is what I see

reflected in the dog's soft, brown eyes
when he & I are both distraught
over a spilled bowl of water.

As a bachelor at 36, I *work things out*
as a courtesy to appease those who dumped me.
I'm a bachelor at 36 so I sleep as long as

I want, with whomever I want.
Dog, TV, internet, birds—
they are my friends & family now,

which is why I weep over the crushed birds
the dog leaves on the pillow.
I find joy again discovering how much

I never knew I love architecture.
I am a bachelor at 36,
& don't have enough time to kill

before I realize there's always time to kill
when something better is feasible
only to those of a certain age.

That body I see in the mirror isn't
the same on the other side;
those antithetical sound bites—

bright water & dumb as a bowl of mice—
I use them to prove I, too, can be a mysterioso
no one but me understands,

the same as when I say *nevertheless* to appear
unconcerned with premonitions—
that as a bachelor at 36 I'm getting closer

to the freedom usually reserved for the dead.
So I gaze into the black & white night
wishing for something to have me,

perhaps the colorless pines
in the valley, or the vegetables
struggling in the soil imploring

my aid—the dirt beneath
my fingernails evidence I couldn't
successfully claw them out.

I am a bachelor at 36.
No one ever need measure my life
in terms of how many missteps it took

for me to get here. I just got lost
along the way
somehow.

~
Part III
~

If You Can't Be Free, Be a Mystery
after Rita Dove

We never knew what to call him, exactly.
So we invented a name exactly
the way we remember him leaving

after Sunday church service when he walked
many blocks home after Sunday church service,
smiling gracefully as he approached us &

as he passed us by, ignored us gracefully
like the hem of his dress swishing
when he approached us then passed us by,

which dazzled us, which we found strange,
so we studied him, the brisk tapping
of his high-heeled shoes we studied

him until his heels vanished into hard
silence & we'd run back to play in the yard,
to poke fun at new names for him

as this was how we ran back to play
in the yard the last time we saw him leaving Odd
Fellows cemetery after Sunday church service,

just as he did the first time we saw him
after Sunday church service entering Odd
Fellows cemetery to escape his mortality,

& perhaps to embrace his immortality,
when we confronted him about his name,
he refused to give us his name.

As Boy at the Elder's Knee, I Come to Understand *Hallelujah*

When a boy's drowning, he tells me, son, it's best
he doesn't frighten easily or

fight the hands tugging him deeper into the eddy.
Let the limbs

go slack as the water
embraces his body

as if he were at home in his mama's arms.
He tells me, let the river make him

part of it... drowning is after all
an existence. & therein lies

my confusion with what's glib & what's wise,
sitting at the elder's knee after church scratching my head as if

shaking a fist at god. I want to ignore him when

he says, *boy, whether during his life*
or after, the dead will be celebrated in the lives of others,

but as a child I don't want to believe in dying,
but to expect failure

in-between the successes, & the further failures
to come—

catharsis that makes a boy precocious
amongst his peers.

I turn to walk away
& he grabs the crook of my elbow

as if to determine the size of the joint,
to marvel

at the skin casing my bones,
though what he's imparting

is the reality of death, of dying, that
it's like fire, he says,

it doesn't burn what it consumes,
it celebrates it.

And Hallelujah for that, his wife says,
having arrived fanning herself, & each of us grows silent

like a soft murmuring after the preacher's sermon
when he says, *Now let us all pray,*

& we bow our heads, our eyes shut tight,
not praying, but wandering the dark cave of our minds,

determined to know
if everything we've ever been told is true.

Story

No one knew for sure if he was   *like that,*
only presumed, wondered why he trekked
fourteen miles to the lake's edge,
alone at night & sat, one pant leg rolled
to his knee, the other bent crooked & wading.
His naked feet—calloused, walk-weary—slid
across pebbles, music of small tides
ebbing to shore lulled him to sleep.
He dreamed of two bodies huddled cheek
to cheek, hip to hip, arms grazing, hands
entwined, walking down this dark street. Bodies
whispered, threw back their heads, opened
their mouths wide & laughed. Sound
rushed down this empty road, eased
under doors, tapped against plate-glass windows,
raised bodies formerly tucked away in bed.
Newly opened eyes searched for the sound
that wrestled them from their dreams.
Fumbling in darkness, bracing themselves
on bedposts, hands pulled back curtains,
twisted blinds open. Eyes red-rimmed
squinted into the night. All was still.
Miss Minnie, Sgt. Dukakis, even
little Samantha witnessed two pairs of arms
wrap around tight, muscular brown bodies
bathed in crescent light, tilt their heads.
Closer. Lips lingered, caressed, tongues
bearing the silence away. From her bedroom
window, Miss Minnie gripped the seams of her
curtains. Sgt. Dukakis sucked his teeth,
restrained the bile rising in his stomach.
Little Samantha watched
(bewildered, tears streaming her face)
her brother kissing the boy next door.
The morning chirping wakened him.
He clambered for the water's edge,
splashed his face, remembered the dream,
gazed at this face bobbing, desperate
to distinguish his tears from the lake's.

The Ghost the Night Becomes

Tonight a boy is lost,
his shadow the only companion
sharing moonlight along the stretch
of dirt road. Away from this boy
the road dusts & winds, & where
he travels, it collects flakes of him.
He wonders how he got to this place,
wonders how his body slips between brush
not wide enough to avoid gnarled branches.
& one hand crosses the other as if to soothe
the pain as one tree fallen in the forest
shoulders another. He walks deeper
into this dark place, whimpering
as a child does, hands braced before him.
Beneath his feet, twigs bend & break
a trail behind him, & somewhere
some living thing cocks its ear & knows
that in his forest a boy is lost, & the trail he's making,
some dead thing is covering it up.

Eclogue on the Death of Eddie "Gwen" Araujo
for the family

By the time I slip into bed
I will have saved in my memory
                    the wet dark boughs,

skeletal looming slant against a gemstone
sky. Birds perched on leaf-less
                    branches sing a weeping chorus.

& while she lay there dying,
did she feel slick black grass
                    against her cheeks?

Did forest creatures
gather in moonlight procession
                    behind her body dragged

across the wooded floor, a halo of
                    leaves & needles collecting

around her head? Did her eyes see past shadows,
                    beyond whirling fists
into the evil of men?

Questions tremble like the low
                    moaning of cello strings.

No one would feel her bulk
shudder the grave they placed her in,
                    know the pain she did not feel yet

kept coming &
coming
& coming.

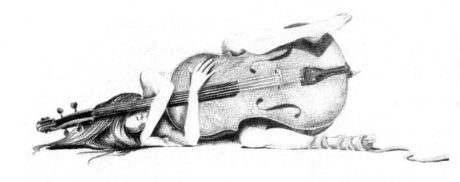

The Cellist's Lament
for Matthew Shepard

Even now this thing of wood grain,
     catgut stretched taut,
          fingerboard that made indentations

in the flesh, the soundpost
     & tuning peg
          tuned to the final note of Barber's *Adagio for Strings*

is still nothing more than a cello.
     How quickly a mind forgets
          music of a bow on strings,

how, as the preacher proclaims,
     you, too, Matthew, are forgotten,
          despite many ears to the ground,

perhaps to distinguish one howling voice from another,
     perhaps to hear voices whisper:
          we bury not only the dead but the living.

I embrace this instrument
     as if it were your body dying
          in a forest of no trees, only leaves

to prove they once existed,
     the way your body pressed blades of grass,
          warmed them, & was evidence you breathed

& lived with no human sounds,
     only a bike riding toward you, the spokes
          wires of a cello, & the wind through them

a bow, your eyes fading
     like the quiet music
          of a note held too long diminishing.

I pluck strings like strands of your hair.
     Music sweeps across the sidewall
          as my hand brushes along curves,

as one would after curtaining hair behind an ear,
    allowing fingers to trace
        contours of a chin, a neck—your face.

But, alas, the *dénouement*:
    a coffin, a grave—
        a cello's case open beside me.

Morehouse College: November 3, 2002

Morehouse sophomore charged in bat attack...
—The Atlanta Journal-Constitution

Was it like sex the way the bat
caused you to bend & writhe
beneath water pouring from a shower
head, rivulets of your blood
whirling down the drain? Or music?

I imagine myself in a stall,
tingling to the very edges of my skin.
Symphony of a thousand thousand violins
in my ear, every syncopated beat
thrums of a bat. Music, & only music,

like orgasm, my arms   eighth notes,
chest   thirty-seconds, mouth   grace notes.
When it ended there was afterglow, a cadence to this opus.
Where did the music go? Was it all metaphor?
The player & instrument evaporated into steam & haze?

for Gregory Love

Swan Song
for Tyler Clementi

A young violinist is to perform his final solo
on a bridge, his hair falling into his eyes.

What to do but rake it back with a trembling hand
while strangers in cars rush by to be with friends

in the city while a sky gone mauve stretches clouds
into one long brow, fall approaching &

the wind a trifle breezier
hence dogs with tongues lolling

from windows but he doesn't notice
& places one hand over the other

to balance his knees on the rails,
loses footing since he can't see.

He bends forward pulling fingers through hair resting
at the nape of his neck,

resting to assure himself composure
how to take one leg over & ease

his heels onto the margin of the bridge with just enough room
to part his hair without falling, just yet,

taming a few stubborn wisps he's always had
to tape behind an ear with a bit of spit

& pressure. He's almost ready, cloistered
in a nook he's sidestepped several paces to find

& thinks of nothing except how to do this
better than all those who've failed before,

how wind makes sails of a shirt
when one hurls through air like a kite tethered to brick.

He doesn't care if the river shatters
when he breaks surface, if he'll crumble

like an ancient cathedral or sink in slow motion
as fish circle like a maypole.

If this doesn't work he can always struggle
through water tugging every finger & limb

fibulae & nail, follicles,
until he's reaching shore digging through mud,

striving toward the nearest thing he can clench in his fists.
He wants to be deliberate for once,

despite tears in his eyes like stars glistening,
a sparkle that dims to a glint

of self-assuredness as if he's guessed the correct answers
on a math quiz, has figured how to wrap his body around a pole

that plunges to the bottom of the river, inch his way to the top
remembering the particulars of geometry, physics, calculus

until his way up equates. But how close to god
before he's disbelieving in heaven again,

to be where the wind diminishes when he reaches
the height closest to a bright angling

beam of moonlight & he sees clearly
the brow of cloud once reflected in the river

has disappeared & the river is now once more
a peaceful wrinkling.

In Defense of the Closet

Who really needs to know the missing part of his story,
        what's there locked behind the eyes, cowering—
                the unsolvable riddle. Something grave peers,
        blank like slate or tombstone chipped away
until only by some generous light what is spelled out
        is barely understood. Why into the eyes do we
                cast down our buckets? Why not into the hands
        which bear the markings of minimal labor, as if
simply from a responsibility to rise from bed
        each morning? Give me his head, the mop of hair
                in which fingers tread strand by strand
                to get to the crown at the center. Remove it
& he'll fall out of his skin, roll in the dirt,
        dip in water, a new casing, entombed, embalmed
                with new life. The missing part is the ragged
        edges where the seams come together, smoothed.
Particles of matter, which is the soul, the better part
        of the body which makes it whole, identifiable,
                lie piled on the floor like rubble of ancient ruins.
        Allow him this dust & you'll find a man who trusts
his own instincts enough to blink without fear
        of being found out. Allow him mystery without
                acknowledging the ghostlier self, to peer
        as if from a window, waiting for the time when
& for whom he will open the door, cross the threshold,
        or to remain locked inside, indefinitely, for the sake of himself.

Blue Silk Robe

for Samuel Alfred Guydon, Sr.
1928-1997

When I think of the end of my life, I hope
it comes slowly as unraveling threads
of Granddaddy's blue silk robe. Leisurely
as his sitting in the early morning hour
eating a plate of peppered cucumbers & tomatoes
glazed with oil & vinegar, remembering stories
he told his grandchildren about singing
The Lord's Prayer on the radio.
I reminisce the day after he died: crept
through his window, crossed dusty seams
like a seasoned robber, slipped in & out
shadowed rooms, hand against my face,
shielding light the way he might have done before or
after he died. I found his robe
strewn across the countertop as if thrown in haste.
Last act before death. I traced the outside seams.
Felt the cold silk against my fingertips.
I entered through the sleeves, bearing the weight
of the robe on my back. I prayed to be swallowed.
To be the silk-like skin hanging from his bones.

Mors Praematura
for Joseph Leroy Guydon, Sr.
1966-2012

... about how Uncle Joe's cancer had advanced
& the news arrived in Mama's face

not with tears alone but her eyes erased
of light, replaced with the abject sadness

of a sister grieving. She stood in
the doorway to my bedroom

as I labored at the computer attempting
a poem, a fiction, an essay—

if I was writing anything at all,
whatever it was was still in

infancy... embryonic or something
like that. All I remember is I tried

hard to appropriate language
with apt metaphors when she arrived

with news of cancer, meaning
her brother was dying.

What I heard was a platitude,
a sound bite embedded in commercials

endorsed by medical associations to warn us.
I was angry. She said *cancer*

so I thought the astrological sign;
she said *cancer* so my mouth watered

for a steamed feast of Alaskan King Crab Legs
dipped in butter; she said *cancer* so my skin

shuddered imagining diseases
you get by fucking

without a condom; she said *cancer*
including the one

where I envisioned the firmament—
meaning we would be attending church

in my bedroom, slugging our way
to the altar for grace, bartering for his life

as if we were his proxy,
knowing how weak he'd become,

his mouth barely able to take in
a sip of water to dissolve the cotton candy

spinning on the loom of his tongue.
In the doorway, Mama

waited for me to reconcile his mortality.
I wanted to pretend nothing had changed:

dinner was still at eight,
the grandchildren had been bathed &

our favorite songs still played
on the stereo in the den. I wanted to

return to writing, figure how to go on
without staring at the cursor blinking

as if it, too, was curious as to what I could say
about the way Mama stood there

poised with news greater than I could bear
when I felt the earth tilt off its axis.

The Sudden End

I wonder how my uncle's wife is getting along
without him. I wonder
if she's hungry or thirsty

for a glass of water; does she feel
it's worth it to unwrap herself
from the afghan she lies on the couch

cocooned inside to go to the kitchen,
take a plate from the cabinet to make a sandwich
or does she forgo the bread altogether

& fold together slices of deli cheese
& salami, spreads them with mayonnaise
rolled up like edible cigars

as she leans against the counter
in her half-darkened kitchen
nibbling deliberately

like a small mouse ear-cocked
to every minor noise & echo
as if she has only a slight chance of vanishing

before anyone can discover her being
normal again? I wonder if she gulps
from the jug of water left all day

on the counter just because.
Does the back door stay unlocked until
she's certain she won't receive

unannounced visitors, mostly
friends & family arriving after work
with their small talk

as if it were a suitcase bulging
with all the great amenities
their lives could never do without?

I wonder if she pours herself a whiskey
& sits in the silent living room
with the flowers wilting & desperate

for water, the stems more woody
than green, as if she intends to grow a tree
in the middle of the room, where she can

lie against it on those days when she simply wants to
draw the curtains, allow in as much sunshine as possible.
But knowing her, it could be gray skies with

only a single crepuscular ray breaking through
the gray clouds & she'd be content with that.
She wouldn't call it a silver lining

but a blessing from god, which makes me
wonder if she can ever listen
to orchestral music from the Romantics,

as I do now, at once thinking of her
& dosing off, fighting against
the bombast of horns & strings like a chorus

of hummingbird wings too close to the ear,
even if she'll never understand
what beautiful creatures those composers made

of notes, how the music exists even in the breath marks
when you have but only a brief moment
to breathe & continue on without

ever feeling the sudden end.

Cracking Lobster

Why would anyone be the last couple lingering
in the corner of a bar, swirling the last sip of wine,
the last hint of crimson that's barely drinkable,
when servers are sweeping their sections,
refilling condiments & the restaurant's closed—
unless their hearts brim with the common minutiae of youth
or they're lovers cheating on their spouses,
placing a chin on the other's shoulder
the way servers know married couples never do in restaurants,
not even on celebratory occasions.
An anniversary dinner is sufficient if a bottle of wine is
shared throughout the meal, a bottle turned upside down
in a wine bucket is a make-shift hourglass when it's time to leave,
to bring the check & dessert to-go, as they need
to relieve the babysitter.
This is what you learn from married couples
while cracking lobster, who ask if you attend the local university,
if this is just part-time work
to give you a sense of responsibility.
You remove the meat from the claws & tail & knuckles
then rake the joints to the edge of a tray,
stuff the tail's shell into the carcass,
presenting the meat, the generous dish of clarified butter
still steaming. You enjoy cracking lobster
especially for these moments, though
you'd rather loosen your tie, fold your apron
& join co-workers for a beer on the patio
because it's what you do in the service industry—
sit around a table just sprayed free of muck
stuck between the table slats & laugh remembering
how you slipped carrying drinks but managed not to spill a drop.
You're hailed a super-server, a model employee,
a person of interest should a lawyer arrive
subpoena in hand for you to testify
because you've witnessed a couple coupling at the bar
who shouldn't have & now it's confirmed.
You think who is this person who's called you to testify?
Perhaps a woman you waited on once,
who sat alone at a small table for two,
in full view of the bar, watching them:
he brushes his nose against her cheek,
she darts a tongue at his earlobe.

You're cracking her lobster as she sits staring,
as if each second ticking by is another room
cordoned off in her heart. You struggle removing the meat,
the carapace having grown so hard you have to hack it apart,
ripping & plying flesh from the walls,
you know so much will remain glued inside the claws
& hope she doesn't mind. You ask if she'd like to
save tomalley leaking from the body,
but she's no longer a woman indulging delicacies,
you presume, sensing how she seems to be rinsed
of a former sweetness evident in how frown lines crowd her eyes
& mouth, what little lasted of youthfulness
vanishing when she tells you *no, take the body away,*
so you do, placing it with the rest of the broken parts
you've collected, leaving a mound of tattered meat
she begins to eat slowly, before you've even packed up
the serving stand & hoisted the tray on your shoulder.
You see her one last time while you're at the tank struggling
so terribly with a lobster you have to snare it with your bare hands.
She passes by not making eye contact, but watches you grab it
by the abdomen to calm its thrashing.
Maybe she turned to witness you walk it back
to the kitchen, to its death. Though, it's likely she left
needing no confirmation, having already known everything
she suspected.

Love, Hate, Apathy

After failing to make love he tells me
the opposite of love is not hate
but apathy. I ask him to let me be.
Is this apathy or a thinner version
of hate? An arm so devoid of nerve
endings one no longer feels
pain. In these moments we know
the vanished limb—no longer there,
we sense its presence & love has lost
its touch. Too much of a good thing.
For the sake of survival it was best
we turned away from each other,
an excuse for pulling & coming together.
No in between.

Self-Portrait as Future Third Person

His face becomes mammal-skin,
        parentheses
drawing shut the eyes.

        When he smiles—
half-moon bags.
        A terrible pallor

courts color
        away on holiday,
across deserts where

        sand dunes become his
shoulders drooped, his back
        a monastery housing

monks weighing him
        in prayers.
Mirrors are a road-

        map to lies—yester-year's—
or what he's come to know
        as the best

of his thighs. This
        is survival of the fit,
though he is the age

        of bovine milk, his body
a heavy stone
        he casts into a well—his

wish to crumble
        like ash, an ember
that burns inside

        out: a star no longer
gaseous
        but a swell

of brittle bones.
        This is the life
he'd live if only

he could sleep
a thousand years,
        awakening when cows came

to pasture
        beside primroses
the color of after-

        glow. This allies him
to simple pleasures
        he'll plant like wild

flowers in the flesh
        that will soon become
soil, a field blossoming,

        a harvest. The reason
he remembers to breathe.

Late Aubade

I've prepared a dinner of your favorites, my sweet,
my darling. Sautéed portobello mushrooms,
scallions, garlic. Baked halibut—white & flaky—
& shrimp in succulent brown butter. Table is set
with plumes of smoke rising from puddles
of trembling wax, the fine china. Sauvignon Blanc
glistens in crystal beneath fluorescent light,
&, for you dearest, I've left the door slightly ajar to invite you in
with these aromas. But when it's too long
I've not heard the hinges creek, I stand outside
in the street mistaking each passing car for yours,
taillights glowing around the bend. I wonder if
you've forgotten me because, baby, we never make love,
seldom kiss, not even a brush against the cheek, hardly
stroke hands whenever your warm body is right here
next to mine. I want to strike across my ruined heart
for not even trying because this half-open door fills
each room with your absence, & what bittersweet is left of you
I want to crawl through & wear.
Simply remembering the shining pearls
of your eyes mocks me with grief, & I fear
we are parting—
though you're not even here.

Elegy

for Jeremy Spring

Each day I spin yarns around my heart.
Lulled to sleep without a body to warm

me, not even a dint in the mattress hints
I've missed a thousand habitual nights of coupling.

If the days weren't so filled with birds'
quick-beat flapping, I may have forgotten the quieter

tenor of fish leaping, flopping mid-air at sea, how
this is the way in which surviving the dead becomes an act

of unkindness. Nodding politely to a woman
carrying her child on hip, I must admit the world does,

indeed, continue to revolve: the moon
cycles & tides excavate rubble, washes it

ashore, I know, just as I know dinner for two
is too much dinner for one. Half the equation is missing—

though my memory of you survives:
you sunning yourself those afternoons hoping

if you perspired toxins would scatter like a flock of crows.
This is how I like to remember you—

not a mattress worn smooth, nor dishes filling a cabinet
with dust. But the sun ravaging you with light,

those birds lost in your body's cast shadow.

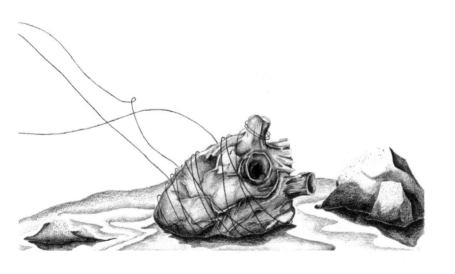

HIV Blues

You hope to get lucky after months
of foolhardy misses, taking
your licks—that is your losses—

in stride as best you can if
your best is to be more profane
than sacred. You've never experienced

the true wham-bam of love,
the turn-me-on-my-ear-&-spank-me
kind of foolishness you drool about

until your face runs like legs
in a swirled glass of wine.
& who said sex & love

were mutually inclusive?
You want sex-beneath-the-bleachers-
after-the-high-school-jamboree

but not the glory-hole
vulgarity, the fingering against the stall wall.
You want a man

who can't finish his flan
because he wants to take you
to the old watering hole,

commit carnal sins,
drive to his home & have you
wait until he's unlocked

the front door before he invites you
in, draws shut the blinds & dims the lights.
Is this an ideal romance

or more like presenting him
your favorite Bordeaux
soured from the sun?

Who'll know until you've swilled
the first sip past your teeth, &
watch the great tragedy unfold.

& how now to coax him—
not ply him,
as that would be indecorous

—into a promenade
where conversation turns casually to sex
since in recent past it's been a train wreck

no one takes their eyes from,
as if it's become the lead story
on the 6 o'clock news,

men in vestibules weeping
because how else to bear
your sex as sarcophagus

for the body? You may as well be
seventeen again, horned up
wishing for tastes of flesh.

You think tonight's the night
to be a letch. If not,
you've lasted all these months now—

never explaining your way
of doing things,
having taught yourself how to be

your own best date so that
no one can woo you better
than you do.

Evensong

I've virtually eliminated myself
a thousand times or more,

      made incubus a rite of passage
      playing the generous host

to lovers-cum-sex partners
who entered the pleasure dome

      in less than full regalia.
      & now I'm stuck with the ick,

a tickle in my throat,
a forced laugh, nervous

      clinking of the glass rim,
      the long long long swallow.

Indecorous behavior indeed
& so I cry *le sigh le sigh*

      & wonder in spite of elimination,
      drunk on pity,

if it's appropriate to pray for
conclusive evidence

      in the sweet hereafter,
      or if god should exist—

let's just get real a moment & ask—
if so, please assume the role of

      an undetectable viral load
      to make my day more thrilling

than The Lady Chablis cameo
sashaying from the beyond

      to give me a reason to kneel down on Sunday,
      examine the risk of transmitting &

praying my blood is no longer a stream
of razor wire,

     but an icicle's gleam
     that drips in abundant sunlight

though never diminishes
as it hangs forever

     a crystal from the branch
     of a cypress in the garden.

& what is a cypress
except the antidote

     so I may again be rooted
     with lips slightly parted,

tongue rapt with the passion
of aphasia, the body spent,

     curled serpentine
     while a face presses hard

against an iced-over window,
warms it & leaves

     its ecstatic impression
     & alas I can believe again

     that a romance can expand eternity,
     two men & a balmy night, heaved

together into a clearing
bejeweled with sweat,

     hour after hour undressing
     night's recriminations.

Since HIV Isn't a Death Sentence Anymore

I find no need for a prayer room
so seldom do I pray, per se, though I do

on occasion pray for
a minor accommodation,

some small want
to be given me

during moments of duress.
Though an activity such as

living with HIV—such stress—
I pray I soon won't be

cursed to death for it,
found in a swallow of earth

sprawled across mulch
& dying leaves slicked to my back,

one leg crossed over the other
as if my last act was to stretch before

a morning exercise
routine or some yoga pose

too many find difficult to hold,
transfixed as a mannequin

toppled over—
all manners of *stillness*

I'd embody, so I pray
I won't go away just yet,

pray I'm not abandoned
to anonymity as if in a snowstorm

with its various degrees of ice
& curious discoveries found

along the way: a single glove,
a loosed scarf swept by the wind

tangled in a stiff high branch,
a jacket inside out as if

removed in haste, socks & shoes
askew, the mated glove found

farther away by a stranger
searching for his dog lost

in the layers of frost he prays
he won't find it likewise

in a snow bank like this—
like this I'm reminded

why I pray less about death
since HIV isn't a death sentence

anymore.
There's still plenty of time

to gaze at constellations
to find my astrological sign in that quadrant

& his in the other.
I will pray for that modicum

of nothing special,
turn fairy tale to true romance

when the real thing can't be found
in real life,

inside this crowded sky
with its scant luminosity

where so many can't discern
one cluster of stars from the next.

I'll take it however I can
—this ignorance—

make the incomprehensible
a recitation each night,

a few quiet words
to warm my cold cupped hands,

which isn't a prayer, per se,
but a recompense.

After learning I'm undetectable, it's as if I've never seen trees breathing on the mountaintop in the distance

& so my limbs slacken
as if I'm crossing a threshold
into a brand-new house
barely able to turn the key
in my new keyhole that opens
a new door into a home so
desperately empty yet utterly
pristine with its white walls &
aroma of lemon-scented
Pine Sol, but also the lingering
gloss of linoleum scrubbed clean,
each cranny like a dried-out ravine
I become almost devastated
to the point of a nervous breakdown
as if somehow I could in an instant
lose it all, the beauty of the well-kept
oak cabinetry, fluorescent glow
inside the ceiling's frosted globe
light fixtures, three bedrooms
any one of them I can choose
to belong only to me but especially
the windows so abundant all I can relish
is the possibility of so much
natural light rousing me as I wander
each room all day until day falls away
like a scab until what's left is the vibrant
wound of night with its stars & moon
& haze of mountaintops pulsing
with all these breathing trees
in the distance that surely come
each evening I'll be beholden,
raising the blinds to lean in
so close to the pane my breath will appear
parceled against glass as if the last
breath I'll ever take, this breath
condensing like tears on the glass,
like dew falling from tree leaves
to the grass I'll feel slick against
the soles of my bare feet whenever
I step outdoors marveled by a kernel
of want fleshed out to a full-bloomed

sensation to live in this house forever,
even if an empty space still in need
of furniture, a perennial wreath
to hang on the door, a WELCOME
mat large enough for as many
visitors as I can stand.

Threat of a City About to Bear a New World

A man in army gear grazes my hand as he rushes by,
turns his head back to wink, & now I'm after him

& his come-hither eye-play I suppose is
an apology. I fight the crowds lined along the street

as if waiting for a parade to begin when there is
none, not to mention the drunks stepping out

from bars for a quick cigarette
because everyone inside's long been fed up

arriving home dressed in malodorous snoods
of smoke netting their hair, lurking around

their necks, spilling from their pockets—
the kind of smoke that, if it could, would speak out of turn

like servers at a dinner party. I should be
after these drunks, not some strange man. & now

I'm halted, again. By a duck crossing the
intersection. It looks both ways, waddles

carelessly between the fender/bumper
of two cars & not even a gasp

of bewilderment from any other passerby—
not even a small child leaning over the side

of his car seat to rap a small fist against the window
crying *Look Mommy! Look Daddy!*

Even the drunks who always have something
to say can only laugh into their own belches,

oblivious. The world is often
cruel in this way, as when said servers dance

in the quarter-dark of the kitchen bowery while blue-
bloods sit around a piano wrangling a song

they've long forgotten, but are nevertheless content
with their snifters & foul-stenched cigars,

& neither the servers nor blue-bloods bear
an understanding of the deeply grievous tragedy

of their stations. But I digress. I'm a traveling one-man
circus trying to spot fatigues wending through crowds

gathering beneath an overcast sky, tenting
raggedy clusters of trees buried in crabgrass

or jagged blocks of cement with its gravelly residue.
I forget what my intentions are in the first place.

All day I've trudged through a relentless gravity.
The air has turned vaporous in the heat,

smoldering licks which could sear the meat off the bone.
I could walk on & on to the edge of the city

if only to forget it—& not even stop at the border,
to turn back. I could forge on & someday I might

arrive at a forgotten city, climb into its cradle
& incubate below a single glowing light.

ACKNOWLEDGMENTS

This book would not have been possible without the institutional support of the departments of English at Tennessee State University and the University of Tennessee-Knoxville, the Bucknell Seminar for Younger Poets (now the Bucknell Seminar for Undergraduate Poets) at Bucknell University, and the Michener Center for Writers at the University of Texas at Austin.

My eternal gratitude to my friends and colleagues who read and offered generous support on early drafts of these poems: josé angel araguz, Sarah Colvert, Kris Bronstad, Amy Boutell, Jenny Browne, Abe Louise Young, Elia Zashin, Tom Nurmi, Matthew Dickman, Michael Dickman, Mike McGriff, Melissa Morrow, Tim O'Connell, Robert Sanchez, Tom Nurmi, Josh Morison, Greg Koehler, Amanda Frost, Abraham Burickson, Sarah Smith, Jake Adam York, Rebecca Wadlinger, and Jibade-Khalil Huffman.

To my teachers Art Smith, Marilyn Kallet, Sandra Bishop Ebner, Paula Closson Buck, Ron Mohring, Shara McCallum, James Harms, Terrance Hayes, David Wevill, Michael Adams, Naomi Shihab Nye, Hayan Charara, A. Van Jordan, and Jack Gilbert, your guidance has done the most.

My eternal gratitude to the G.O.A.T. poets Donika Kelly, Ansel Elkins, Dexter L. Booth, Carol Guess, and Denise Duhamel for vouching for me.

My eternal gratitude to the G.O.A.T. artists Annie Fletcher for her illustrations and Shelly O'Barr for her inspired rendering of Joshua McKnight's magnificent photo, "Two Men Touching Forehead."

And this book would never have been possible if not for Jesse Graves, who made it his life's mission to bring back into print the poems gathered in my three chapbooks. This book comprises most of those poems. Of course, Jesse was not alone in this venture. I am also indebted to Sappho Stanley's astute and invaluable suggestions for revising three chapbooks into a unified collection. And not least of all, thank you to Denton Loving at EastOver Press for his blind faith in this project.

And to my daddy, Clarence Stewart; my mama, Felicia Guydon Stewart; my brother, Carlos Stewart; and my sister, Jakia Stewart. My first family.

I also gratefully acknowledge the editors of publications in which the following poems appeared in either their original or slightly different forms:

Anti—: "Self-Portrait with Dog"
Appalachian Review: "As a Boy at the Elder's Knee, I Come to Understand *Hallelujah*"
Assaracus: "In Defense of the Closet," "A Tryst"
Bloom: "Self-Portrait in Atlanta, Georgia"
Callaloo: "Cracking Lobster," "Statues in the Park"
Chelsea Station Magazine: "After learning I'm undetectable, it's as if I've never seen the trees breathing on the mountaintop in the distance"
Cider Press Review: "The Terribly Beautiful"
Cimarron Review: "Murophobia," "The 'Keep It on the Down Low' Rhythm & Blues Show"
Fifth Wednesday Journal: "My Mother's Hands"
Gertrude: "Aftermath"
Knockout: "Auguries: A Love Story" (as "Auguries of Digression: A Love Story")
Lodestar Quarterly: "Epithalamion" (as "Four-Part Epithalamion")
Many Mountains Moving: "Self-Portrait as Future Third Person"
Meridian: "Troubled Lovers"
New Millennium Writings: "Even Bones," "Story"
Our Time Is Now: "Eclogue on the Death of Eddie 'Gwen' Araujo," "Morehouse College: November 3, 2002," "Saleem & Son's Barbershop" (as "Barbershop")
Paper Street: "The Cellist's Lament"
Pebble Lake Review: "Myopia"
Poet Lore: "After Rene Magritte's 'The Lovers'"
Potomac Review: "Delirium Tremens," "My Father Walks in Rain with No Umbrella"
storySouth: "Communally Bound," "The Ghost the Night Becomes," "Intimacies in Borrowed Light," "The Sudden End"
The Good Men Project: "A Bachelor at 36," "Mors Praematura" (as "Mors Praematura (a story))"
The Pinch: "Because I Have Something to Say" (as "Leitmotif")
The Seattle Review: "Driftwood"

"Blue Silk Robe" appeared in *di-vêrsé-city: 2005 Anthology of the Austin International Poetry Festival* as "To Be"
"Driftwood" and "The Terribly Beautiful" appeared in *The Southern Poetry Anthology Volume VI: Tennessee*
"Elegy" appeared in *Best Gay Poetry 2008* ; *Tupelo Press Poetry Project* as "Snails, Worms, and Other Losses"
"Ennui" appeared in *A Tapestry of Voices: An East Tennessee Anthology*
"The Ghost the Night Becomes" appeared in *storySouth: The Best of the South 2005; The Southern Poetry Anthology Volume III: Contemporary Appalachia*
"My Mother's Hands" and "Statues in the Park" appeared in *The Southern Poetry Anthology Volume III: Contemporary Appalachia*
"Saleem & Son's Barbershop" appeared in *Knoxville Bound: A Collection of Literary Works Inspired by Knoxville, Tennessee*
"Self-Portrait as Future Third Person" appeared in *Verse Daily* ; *The Southern Poetry Anthology Volume III: Contemporary Appalachia*

Several of these poems were also collected in the following chapbooks:

The Terribly Beautiful (2006 Main Street Rag Editor's Choice Chapbook Series):
"After Rene Magritte's 'The Lovers'"; "Aubade" ("If this love…"); "Blue Silk Robe" (as "To Be"); "The Cellist's Lament"; "Driftwood ; "Eclogue on the Death of Eddie 'Gwen' Araujo"; "The Ghost the Night Becomes"; "In the Clair de Lune"; "Late Aubade"; "Morehouse College: November 3, 2002"; "On the Bus"; "Reverb at the Carousel II (as "First Night"); "Saleem & Son's Barbershop"; "Self-Portrait at Eight"; " Self-Portrait in a Thunder- storm"; "Self-Portrait on Key West Auction Block"; "Semantics"; "The Terribly Beautiful"

Sotto Voce (2008 Main Street Rag Editor's Choice Chapbook Series):
"A Tryst"; "Aubade" ("Dearest, we've become"); "Dawn"; "Dusk"; "Elegy"; "Epithalamion"; "Even Bones"; "Intimacies in Borrowed Light"; "Love, Hate, Apathy"; "Myopia"; "Picaresque"; "Prayer"; "Self-Portrait as Recurring Bird"; "Self-Portrait in Atlanta, Georgia"; "Sotto Voce"; "Statues in the Park"; "A Tryst"

The Ghost the Night Becomes (2013 Gertrude Press Poetry Chapbook Contest Winner):
"The Cellist's Lament"; "Communally Bound"; "Eclogue on the Death of Eddie 'Gwen' Araujo"; "Elegy"; "The Ghost the Night Becomes"; "In Defense of the Closet"; "Leitmotif" (as "Because I Have Something to Say"); "Prayer"; "Statues in the Park"; "Story"; "A Tryst"